CATTLE COUNTRY
OF PETER FRENCH

CATTLE COUNTRY
OF
PETER FRENCH

Alturas

OREGON

Ft. Bidwell

Upper Alkali Lk.

Middle A. Lk.

Lower A. L.

1872

Oregon Surprise Valley

to Route

Ft. Crook

Pit River

Old Station

Eagle Lk.

Pine Cr.

Horse Lk.

Redding

Shingletown

Battle Cr.

Lake Manzanita

"n" Lassen Pk.

Fredonia

Susanville

French's Route

Red Bluff

Lake Almanor

OREGON

Lakeview

Oregon area of Peter French's dr.

Peter French's

Sacramento River

Chico

Butte Creek

Feather River

Goose Lake

Willows

Jacinto

Cids Landing No.

Colusa

California area of Peter French's drive

CALIFORNIA

CALIFORN

Goose Lake

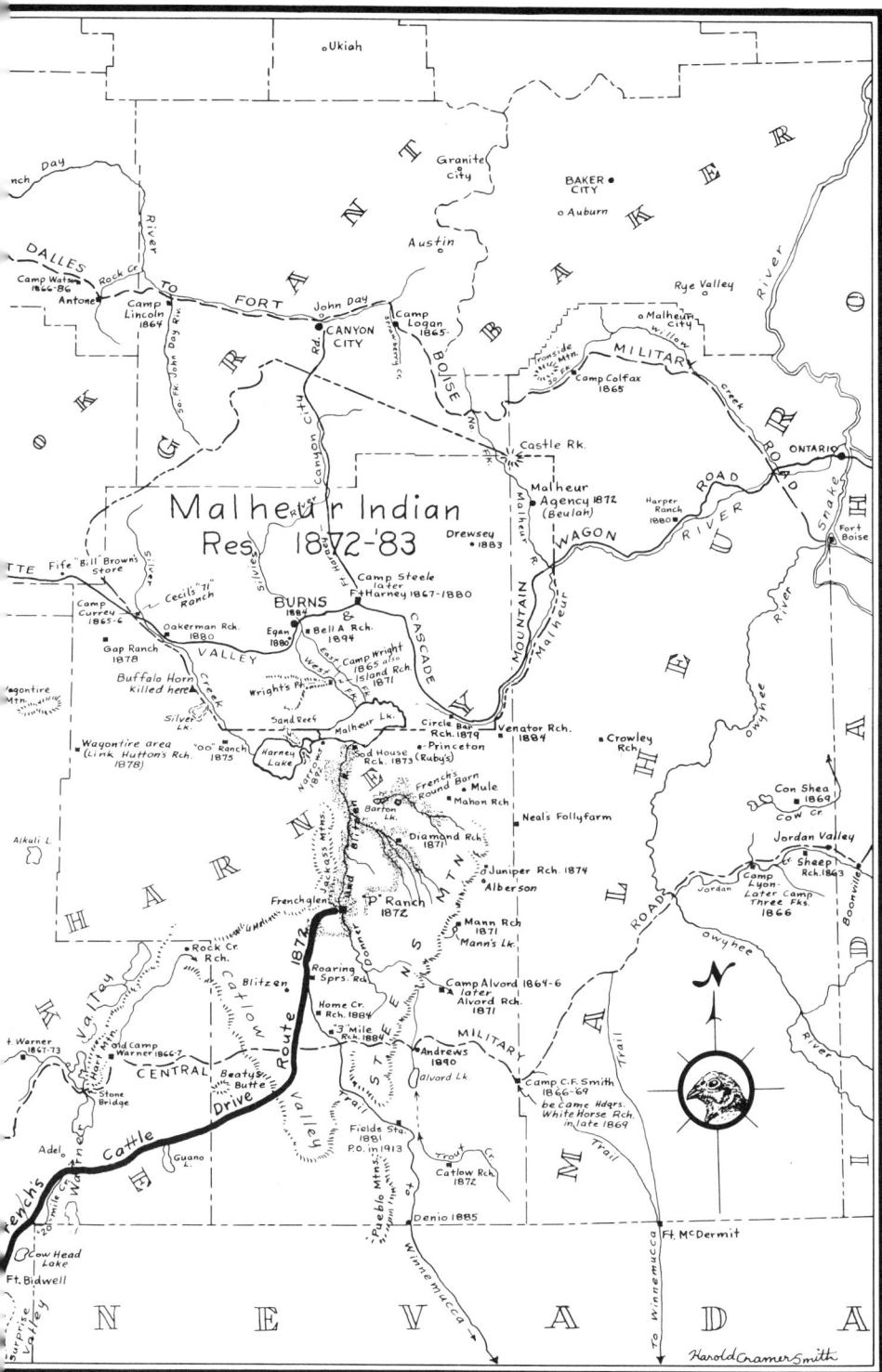

Malheur Indian
Res. 1872-'83

CATTLE COUNTRY

Portland · Oregon ·

# of PETER FRENCH

BY GILES FRENCH

BINFORDS & MORT, *Publishers*

CONTENTS

This book is about Cattleman Peter French and his contemporaries who developed the great stock ranches in Southeastern Oregon in the late nineteenth century. It has been compiled from the records, with an attempt to discard the extravagant yarns that have been told and written about these men of the Old West. They were not heroes or demons; they qualified for neither role. The popular depiction of them is a distorted one. The way they actually lived, the work they did, the equipment they used—all this should be a part of our history, not just of our romantic dreams.

A rider on a cow ranch was a working man. He was hired for his skills. The life he led was hard and sometimes dramatic, but in his day it was no more touched with glamor than pitching hay—which he sometimes did. Those riders were people, not gods on horseback, and they faced the same personal problems as their grandsons, who now daily head for shop or office.

French himself was a person with strong and very definite character traits—some of them laudable, some merely human. He ruled a domain as large as some states while he was developing his vast cattle empire in the Blitzen valley. To this work and to the Glenns, he gave his life.

Although of the same name as my own, Peter French was not a relative. He was of the southern branch of the family; the writer came from Vermont. The reason for this book about him is that it seemed time to portray him as a man, how he met his problems, the forces that brought him down.

No one can write a book of history without the aid of a great many persons and much research. Almost every courthouse, where records might be found about Peter French, has been visited. State historical societies have been consulted. Librarians—the kindest of women—have been unfailingly helpful. Leo McCoy of Red Bluff was of inestimable aid.

GILES FRENCH

THE SOUTHEASTERN QUARTER OF OREGON IS THE romantic part of the state. Here rode the men on horseback, here moved dusty bands of cattle over the sage-covered plateaus. While the mountain peaks looked on, men fought for the land at their feet with every weapon known, from law to guns.

The geography itself is dramatic. From the lakes of the Warner Valley, Hart Mountain rises to over eight thousand feet and slopes to the east; fifty miles farther east the mighty Steens catches the snows. The two ranges are like book ends in reverse position; Hart Mountain's steep side is to the west and the Steens' drop is on the east. Between is a rocky plain, decorated by Beatys Butte and the Catlow Valley. The moisture trapped by the mountains falls on the west side of their summits, making the lake-filled Warner Valley and the Donner und Blitzen Valley, that is the drainage for the Steens. East of the Steens, the Malheur and Owyhee rivers flow to the Snake through deep canyons; and on the north, small creeks and rivers come down from the Blue Mountain range, often flooding the Harney Basin with snow water until June.

Water is an important geographic factor and the major economic resource. All the ranches are located on creeks or rivers; and the battles, actual and legal, were fought over water. To the great cattlemen goes credit for the building of thousands of miles of irrigation canals and ditches—which the smaller ranchers were generally permitted to use.

Harney Valley is dotted with lake beds, formed by the rising Cascades. Some of these lakes evaporated; some discovered outlets; others were choked by volcanic dust. There are a number that contain water during the short rainy period, but many remain dry throughout the year, or retain only enough moisture to become meadows in the summer months.

It is a land of long shadows and far-off horizons—where a man can "look a long way out and a long way up."

There are buttes that thrust their peaks over six thousand feet toward the sky, remnants of some unfamiliar geological formation; there is the Alvord Desert, eight miles wide and fifteen miles long, on which nothing grows, so barren and desolate that few men cross it; there are springs that flow from the rimrock to water a few acres of early-season meadow; there are lakes made acrid by alkali. And there are miles and miles of open country covered with greasewood that shadows the sparse bunchgrass.

On the flats, half hidden by the stiff and stubborn sage, there are the remains of homesteader cabins, built by hopeful and misguided men, and long abandoned. It was never a country for the small landowner; it takes a lot of it for financial security. Here and there are abandoned towns, once prosperous trading centers, with stores, perhaps a dance hall and a saloon, whose populations departed with the homesteaders. Blitzen, Andrews, Follyfarm, Narrows, Mule, Princeton, Alberson and Harney are only memories. It was not an easy land to conquer and, despite the building of modern roads and adequate houses, it is doubtful if many of the present-day residents feel that it has yet been conquered.

The first white men to halt there were members of a party led by Antoine Sylvaille, sent by Peter Skene Ogden to trap beaver along the rivers in 1826. In 1845, an emigrant train blundered through, lost and hungry, to make itself forever remembered by a story of a blue bucket and a nugget-pebbled spring, that has been hunted by optimists for a century. Parties of soldiers came to explore a route for an easily traveled road and to give their names to the physical features of this wide and lonely land. Later they chased the native Indians onto reservations, preparatory to settlement by the white man, who intended to prevail in all the West.

Because the grass grew tall in the meadows and on the watered slopes, cattlemen followed the soldiers to range their stock on the open country that belonged to the Federal government, but, according to custom, was theirs to use. They could not hoard it, nor fence it, and it was only theirs to use while they had cattle to eat the grass and proclaim possession. They were all men as rugged as the country; all first settlers have to be. Their determination was equal to the hardships. Of the four big stockmen who achieved the most prominence and made the most history, all came from California; all were backed by financiers in that state. Without available money they could not have expanded to become the land-and-cattle barons they did.

CATTLEMEN ~~~~~~~~~~~~~~~~~~~~~~~~~~~~~~~

FOREMOST AMONG THESE CATTLEMEN WAS PETER
French, backed by Dr. Hugh James Glenn of Jacinto, who was a
historical character in his own right. There was John Devine, whose
backer was W. B. Todhunter of Sacramento. Henry Miller, perhaps
the shrewdest of them all, had already helped develop the San
Joaquin Valley in California with the aid of Charles Lux, who
knew where to get money. Colonel James Hardin, with the support
of Amos Riley, a storekeeper in Santa Rosa, was an early stockman
whose expansion was toward Wagontire and out of the Harney
Basin.

These were the big cattlemen who controlled wide tracts of
meadow and hill, bought or pre-empted springs, lived like frontier
lords, and worked the clock around to increase their land and cattle,
building their own glory and prestige in conjunction with the financial security of their sponsors.

There were smaller operators, who established themselves on
the ranges and remained for a few years before selling to the bigger
cattlemen. Among them was William Walter Brown—Bill Brown,
Wagontire Brown—whose habits were strange to his contemporaries,
although he was one of them in determination and ruggedness. He
raised sheep and horses around Wagontire Mountain and northward to the Gap Ranch, until the third decade of this century.
When his herders quit, he would throw his bands of sheep together
and herd them himself, staying with them for days with no food
but a pocketful of raisins, sometimes mixed with the strychnine he
used to poison coyotes. He killed Johnnie Overstreet, a herder for

the OO Ranch of Riley and Hardin, after being threatened and fired upon. He then rode to the nearest county seat to report it, and was soon exonerated.

His worst expletive was "Shucks, confound it." This sounded weak among men who regularly called upon the saints and the Deity for support of the most careless statement. Brown wrote his checks on any scrap of paper, and his credit policy for the store he kept at the Gap Ranch was the delight of the indigent homesteaders. He died in a Methodist home he had long helped support in Salem.

Bill Hanley achieved fame as a cattleman and a public figure through ownership of the Bell A and the OO ranches. He came to southeastern Oregon from Jacksonville, when a young man, becoming manager of the P Ranch after the death of Peter French, where he continued the conservation program of the late owner. Hanley was not a permanent resident of the Harney Basin until the 1880s, after he was thirty years old. By living until 1933, he was able to revel in the glamor that came to the cattle business in the twentieth century.

Tom Overfelt was an early stockman with headquarters on the North Fork of the Malheur River, east of the Harney Basin. He was responsible for one of the more dramatic stories that has become incorporated into western fiction. In 1883, the Federal government had abandoned the Malheur River Agency in Southeast Oregon, putting most of the land back into the public domain. The half section on which the buildings were located was put up for bids at the land office in Lakeview. Overfelt heard of it sometime after the posting of the request for bids. He headed at once for Lakeview to present Henry Miller's Bullhead draft in payment.

Miller's Bullhead drafts were common currency wherever he operated. They were a draft on Miller and Lux, similar to drafts of this day; and ranch managers had authority to sign them. They were not written directly on a bank because Miller and Lux used several banks; they were on the firm itself, and they were always good.

However, the draft was refused by the land office authorities at Lakeview. Later the general land office in Washington—at the insistence of Miller who was already backing Overfelt—ruled it a valid payment. Tales are still told of a lone horseman riding almost three days to reach the land office on time. Maurice Fitzgerald, of Fort Harney, said he drove Overfelt to Lakeview in a buggy—which does some damage to a good story.

Overfelt died in 1886, killed by a runaway horse; or, as some said, was shot first by a man who was with him. Miller took over the property by paying Mrs. Overfelt for her interest. John Catlow came from England and mined in southwestern Idaho, where he made some money with which to start a ranch on Trout Creek near John Devine's White Horse Ranch. He fenced it with lumber hauled by A. H. Robie's eight span of oxen from his mill on Rattlesnake Creek, a hundred miles away. Catlow spread out into the valley, later named after him.

In 1866, sometime after Camp Currey was abandoned, Logue Cecil moved to its site on Silver Creek, to go into the stock business. His brother, Carl, joined him. The Cecils also raised mules. This is one of the few old ranches still operated by a descendant of the original owner. J. C. (Pat) Cecil is still in the stock business.

These stockmen of the Steens were spiritual or physical descendants of the American pioneers who had expanded the boundaries of the United States from the Atlantic to the Pacific Ocean. Through the geographical back doors of the original thirteen colonies, pioneers strode westward to the Mississippi, following Lewis and Clark and the fur traders to the Pacific. With the aid of hardy emigrants from Europe, they settled the mountains and plains in between. It was one of the remarkable feats in the history of the human race, this expansion of a people in so short a time.

The men, and the women, who were responsible for it were themselves remarkable, otherwise the job would not have been done. The explorers, the fur trappers, the frontiersmen, and the entrepreneurs who developed the West—as it was snatched, still bloody, from the hands of dead or captive Indians—were all of a kind. They were bold and brave or they would not have ventured into the unknown West. They were inventive and resourceful or they could not have stayed. They were ambitious and wise or they would not have utilized the resources of the new country.

If it had not been for such men and their peculiar qualities of character, the West might still be a battleground between Indians and whites, with its lands unplowed, its timber decaying, its minerals unmined. In the latter part of this golden age of the West, the men who won respect were those who built the transcontinental railroads, who dug the gold and silver to expand the nation's monetary wealth, who cut the timber to build the farm homes and towns, who developed the ranches to make use of the most basic resource of all: the soil.

Every man must be judged by the times in which he lived. The men of the nineteenth century, especially the successful ones, were individuals who planned their own lives, made their own decisions and rose or fell by their own judgments. Their characteristics were bravery, loyalty, and a shrewd, practical intelligence. These settlers of the Steens were not carbon copies and, unfortunately, they left none.

Of these cattlemen, more has been written about Peter French than about any of the others. He lived the most dramatic life; he had the most violent death. He was the best cattleman, had the best ranch, and was the most colorful—and controversial. Peter French was born April 30, 1849, in Callaway County, Missouri, to Marian "Bry" French and his wife, Mary Burt. He was christened John William. The "Peter" came later.

In 1850, Bry French moved to California's Colusa County, one of the twenty-seven original counties of that new state. But finding Colusa County, with its innumerable Spanish grants an inhospitable place for a man of small means, he went on up the Sacramento Valley to Tehama County. On a knoll in the red-soiled area near the Noma Lakee Indian Reservation, he built a substantial two-story house and went into the sheep business, the customary occupation of stockmen in that time and place. The house that stands on that spot is constructed like a fort: heavy planks stand vertical and are strengthened by others placed diagonally, to form solid walls into which shuttered windows and doors are sawed. Containing more lumber than two ordinary houses of the same size, it would have been protection against the fire of the best rifles of the time. Freight teams and, later, stages, pulled past its door on the way to the settlements and towns in the western range of mountains. This traffic brought to young John William a touch of romance and an active interest in far-off places.

He was nine years old before another child was born to the Frenches, Mary arriving in 1858. A much younger son, Burt, was born in 1873, after John William had set out on his own, and adopted the name of Peter.

Bry French was a well respected man in the community. When he died, October 7, 1887, the Red Bluff *Sentinel* described him as "a good neighbor, an upright citizen and highly esteemed by a large circle of friends." Old-timers, whose fathers knew Bry French, recall his memory with respect. He was a man who took an interest in, and had a part in, the affairs of the community.

All the Frenches were small. In truth, most men were smaller a hundred years ago. Peter has never been described as more than five feet, five or six inches, by men who knew him. He grew into his teens, a dark youth with black hair, an extremely large head, and piercing black eyes that were later said to look clear through a man. He was quick of movement and of thought. Whatever he did he gave to it his fullest attention and energy. The work on the comparatively small sheep ranch and the affairs of a small farming community could not contain him long.

WHEN YOUNG FRENCH FELT HIMSELF OLD ENOUGH
to go out into the world to make his own living, he naturally headed
down the Sacramento River toward the center of population and
greater agricultural activity. He entered the employ of Dr. Hugh
James Glenn at Jacinto. An aggressive promoter and fellow Mis-
sourian—known to Bry French in that state and in Colusa County—
Glenn was to become the man to exert the greatest influence on
Peter French; in fact the story of one cannot be told without that
of the other.

Dr. Glenn was born in Virginia, near Staunton, September 18,
1824. He earned a medical degree and served for a time as a doctor
in the Mexican War, but life in the army did not appeal to him.
He resigned his commission to find more profitable adventure. After
his marriage to Nancy Harrison Abernathy—a small and not well-
favored woman—in March of 1849, he bought some livestock and
drove them across the prairies to California, which, in 1849, was
adventure enough for almost anyone. Because the West was short
of domestic stock, he sold his herd for a good price. Gold had been
discovered the year before at Sutter's Mill, and Americans were
flocking to the new land as fast as ships and wagons could take
them. Prices were what the seller dared ask.

Hugh James Glenn was a man about five feet eight inches in
height, erect, aggressive, and red bearded. He did not call himself a doctor, nor did he practice medicine in his mature life, except in emergency. He did not pose as a farmer or a stockman.
Rather, he called himself a trader and gave that as his occupation

when registering to vote. His family consisted of nine children, not all of whom reached maturity. Among them was Ella, born in 1860, and destined to become Peter's wife—and a person of endless controversy.

Glenn was an indulgent father, giving his family everything they asked for, and demanding nothing in return. Because he was seldom home with them, they grew up to be just the kind of children such treatment nearly always produces. None had their father's ability to organize, or accept responsibility. However, all developed his quality of spending money.

In 1849, at the age of twenty-five, Glenn started a lifetime of promotion—the same year that Peter French, who was to be a major instrument of his ambition, was born.

Never tempted into gold digging, Glenn returned several times to Missouri for more stock. He made at least a dozen trips, bringing cattle, horses and, on one occasion, sheep to the new country. He was successful enough to establish himself as a promoter of promise, known to money lenders and business men in San Francisco. That booming city was the center of mercantile activity for the mines in California and Nevada; its foremost citizens piled up early fortunes, selling supplies to the miners who were willing to pay high prices for the picks they swung and the bacon they ate. The gold fever was on and men must dig.

The one-time doctor allied himself with those who took their gold second-hand and certain. He was bold and resourceful, with nerve to tackle any proposition that promised a good return. In 1867, he was living in Yolo County, on Putah Creek, where he was in partnership with S. E. Wilson, who had married Mrs. Glenn's sister. But Glenn was looking for a larger opportunity.

Such an opportunity came in November of that same year, when he found he could buy a part of the Jacinto grant, some seven thousand acres of land lying in northern Colusa County, which the heirs of the original Spanish owner would not farm and could not retain. Their way of life did not include attention to agriculture. Wealth had made them accustomed to—and adept at—spending, not earning; and they had to sell to the hungrier, more ambitious Americans. Nearly all the Spanish grants were bought for similar reasons, as the influx of new residents into California raised the price of land far above its value to the luxury-loving Spaniards. The United States had obtained possession of California in 1848, by treaty with Mexico, and its citizens soon acquired actual ownership of the land.

The price of the Jacinto grant was $1.60 per acre, which in this day seems moderate enough. For $11,200, Dr. Glenn owned a tract of level land, adjacent to the Sacramento River, that would graze a sizable herd of cattle or sheep. He was able to borrow such funds as he needed for the purchase, as well as for improvement and expansion.

Glenn's career for the next fifteen years was one of the most fabulous in the history of all California. The doctor soon increased his holdings by buying the remainder of the Jacinto, along with other grants. He raised horses and mules and cattle, until he discovered that the broad river bottom would grow wheat, which was in demand to make the flour needed for the population of the ever-growing state. Before long, he earned the reputation of being the biggest wheat grower in the western world. Newspapers hailed him as the Wheat King, especially after 1879, when a bumper crop on his 45,000 acres yielded a million bushels.

Dr. Glenn was a great builder. It was said that he had thirty-eight houses, twenty-seven barns and fourteen blacksmith shops on his ranch, and that his gang plows traveled all day in a straight line, so long was his ranch. He was always building and buying houses, barns, sheds, warehouses, stores, and the machinery needed to cultivate his acres. Farm machinery was then crude and heavy, and as there was not even much of it in the West, Glenn imported it from the eastern states, buying in quantity, and having it specially built. He had the advantage of developing the ranch according to his own ideas, no one before having laid out any fields or erected any buildings. It was all new.

Among Glenn's first constructions was a magnificent residence near what is now Cid's Landing, on the west bank of the Sacramento River, east and north of Willows, a town that came into being largely because of the development of the Jacinto Ranch. The house was finished in the ornate style of the period, with no thought of expense. The doctor was on the way up and intended that his home reflect his position and his ambition. His home was not only a residence, but an advertisement of his success—as were many of the big homes built by prosperous first settlers. It had three stories and twenty-two rooms, many of which boasted marble fireplaces to heat the high ceilings that were the fashion. There were porticos, tall windows, and carved woodwork. The marble came from Italy. The masons and carpenters were from San Francisco, and they were given a free hand to decorate the house to the best of their ability.

The grounds were adorned with trees of many kinds, some brought from long distances, and they were planted in a wide lawn where several hundred persons could recline in the shade and be regaled with cooling drinks or more stimulating refreshments. It was altogether a home befitting a man who had set out to become a commercial king.

Between the big house and the river, Dr. Glenn built a huge brick warehouse, which became the office and store for the ranch. Here were dispensed the tobacco and clothing that several hundred men had to buy there, or do without. Here were written the orders for machinery and repairs as well as for the endless supplies needed in the vast enterprise. This was headquarters. Around and about were the barns to shelter the thousands of horses and mules that were used to till the fields. Here were the corrals where new animals were broken to ride and work, and here were the bunkhouses of the workers.

Today the Glenn mansion stands a wreck, covered with overgrowing vines and shadowed by the trees that once decorated it. Its windows are broken and decay is evident throughout. Chickens wander through its many rooms, clucking and making nests in the marble fireplaces where once ladies discreetly warmed their shins and men dropped ashes from imported cigars. The present farmer of the land lives in a modest house nearby, disdaining the once-festive mansion.

The practice at Jacinto was to hire Mexican and Chinese labor, likely because it was cheaper and more easily managed. The Americans who came to the West in the middle years of the nineteenth century were an independent lot who preferred to do something for themselves rather than work for others, especially for those whose disciplines were strict. Foreign labor was steadier, less independent. However, foremen—of whom the ranch never had enough—were usually Americans, experienced with horses and men.

Colusa County was in the process of change. It had been grazing land before Glenn plowed some of it and began raising good crops of wheat. Others followed suit until stockmen had no place to run their cattle and sheep. Many stockmen owned little land, running their animals on the public domain—as was the custom in nearly all of the West. But the public domain was rapidly becoming private land. There was demand for meat, but there was a greater demand for flour. So great was the need for food that there was more money to be made in agriculture than in grazing.

Some cattlemen, as a result, began to move away from Colusa County, as well as other counties in the Sacramento Valley. Glenn himself had bought a cattle spread in Paiute Valley, Nevada, which he stocked in parnership with E. Waller Crutcher, who was to receive a third of the increase for his services as manager. Descendants of Crutcher say the venture was not successful and he made nothing from it.

The big stockmen were none too quick. California politicians, like politicians everywhere, were responsive to the majority, and the new men flocking to the Golden State wanted land for themselves. This meant the end of open-range cattle grazing along the Sacramento River.

On March 28, 1872, the legislature approved a law, marked formally as CCLVIII, which specified that within thirty days there should be made a list of brands in each county and that justices of the peace should all receive a copy. Thereafter, it was decreed, "any owner or occupant of land, whether or not enclosed, may take up and safely keep, at the expense of the owner, any animal found trespassing upon said land. He shall be allowed for each day, 20 cents for cattle, 10 cents for hogs, and five cents for sheep, and damages." The description of the animals was to be posted.

No stockman could operate under such a law, and presumably that is what the legislators intended, or at least is what the backers of the bill intended. It meant that any man, landowner or lessee, could take up stock and hold them for damages and feed. This was at a time when cattle were being grown on the open range in Montana and Wyoming for a dollar or two a year, which made the six dollars a month for care of impounded cattle, plus damages, an impossible hazard. Furthermore, enforcement was in the hands of the small property owner or resident, who might feel the need for a little extra income. Posting could easily be done in some inconspicuous place that the stockman would not notice—until the bill was large enough to suit the holder of the stock.

California cattlemen now began looking toward Oregon for new grazing lands. They had read about the victories of General George Crook, when he drove the Indians back to their reservations up in that state; and after the Civil War, the army lost little time in corralling the Paiutes and Bannocks that had got out of hand when Federal troops were removed to fight the war. Local detachments had been ineffective against them. By the late 1860s, army forts had been established at Bidwell in Surprise Valley, at Warner on Honey Creek, and at Harney, near the mouth of Rattlesnake Creek, at the foot of the Blue Mountains. There were also numerous camps from which a body of troops could operate when necessary. The troublesome Paiutes were on the Malheur River Reservation in Grant and Baker (now Harney and Malheur) counties, and the Bannocks were on a reservation in Idaho. Chief Winnemucca, grown old and peaceable, and his daughter, Sarah, once a white man's bride, wanted them to stay there. Everything considered, Oregon seemed a suitable place to which cattle could be moved.

Contrary to rumor and some writers, it is doubtful if Dr. Glenn or the other stockmen who moved to Oregon knew about the Oregon Swamp Act. The Oregon legislature did not pass an enabling act for acquisition of swamp land until 1870, and it was 1872 before filings were reported in official documents.

Glenn had been glad to be able to hire Peter French when that young man came down from Tehama County. He set him to breaking horses at Jacinto. Peter had grown up on a ranch, knew stock, was of the disposition to work for his employer's interests, and was an ally of the boss instead of a mere employe. Because within a few months he became a favorite of the Mexican vaqueros and teamsters, he was made a foreman in charge of them. Peter learned to speak their language; he earned their respect.

Those who knew Peter French well, respected him and trusted him implicitly. No other cattleman engendered such loyalty among his crew; no other cattleman gave so much loyalty to his friends. He was a man who offered full assurance of protection and aid, of physical and spiritual support. Because strong men have strong friends and strong enemies, persons outside French's circle of friends sometimes became enemies; but they did not lose their respect for his abilities.

French could get things done. The abilities of Dr. Glenn did not run to detail—at which French was particularly adept. Glenn liked French, and the younger man learned the elder's strategy and tactics. He made Glenn his economic and spiritual godfather.

By 1872, French had been in the Glenn employ for two or three years and seemed content to remain. He had registered to vote in Colusa County when he became twenty-one, giving his name as Peter (probably bestowed on him by the Mexicans), instead of the John William his parents had christened him. He appeared a likely young man, with too much integrity to steal, and too much loyalty to branch out for himself after a few years of working for another. He had just turned twenty-three, age enough for added responsibility in that century when Americans matured young.

As grazing lands became scarcer, Glenn found it necessary to move his cattle from Jacinto; he did not want to sell them, for the cattle business was profitable. Like some of the other large stockmen, he decided to expand into Oregon. To head the drive, he selected young Peter French. There is no reason to believe that Glenn sent French to Oregon with twelve hundred head of grade Shorthorn cows, some better bulls, and about twenty saddle horses, with any other intent than to expand his business and make a profit.

To intimate that Glenn was motivated by a sentimental attachment to the young man—who had already proved his ability to handle men and stock—is to misunderstand the doctor; he acted almost entirely from self-interest. Besides, French showed promise of having the aggressiveness, the organizational ability, and perhaps the ruthlessness to be a success in a new territory. The risk was comparatively small; the reward might be manifold, not only in money, but in prestige, which could insure credit and raise the pushing promoter and his family into a position of even higher social and economic standing.

Neither French nor Glenn knew about the region in Oregon where the cattle were to be taken—even assuming that they had decided on the exact location. The problems of climate, grass, and the distance from supplies were to be French's to solve. To him, the move north was adventure; to Glenn it was speculation.

Peter French likely had little contact with the Glenn family while he worked at Jacinto. Except for the doctor himself, it was not customary for the Glenns to associate with the employes; and he did not mingle with them socially. The Glenns lived in the big house and enjoyed themselves as landowners. The sweaty foremen, smelling of horses, did not fit into such company.

Al Monner

The Oregon Steens country, surrounded by sloping hills, where grass grows as high as a man's stirrups, seemed like cattle heaven to Peter French, when he first looked down on it in the summer of 1872.

Catlow Valley Road. This region—named for John Catlow, an early Harney stockman—is part of the country Peter French traveled through when he drove his first California herd north.

Part of the Peter French cattle country, now the home or nesting grounds for millions of wild birds.

Two views of picturesque Harney Lake at the Narrows—the name suggested by the narrow channel connecting Harney and Malheur lakes. Mart Brenton claimed that, when he kicked some sand around at the Reef in the high water period of 1881, he started Malheur draining westward into Harney Lake. Others say the action started from natural causes.

Steens Mountain south of Alvord Ranch. The mountain was named for Major Enoch Steen, who headed a military expedition into Southern Oregon in 1860. The ranch takes its name from the desert, both honoring General Benjamin Alvord, prominent in the early Indian wars of Eastern Oregon.

A small bunch of calves east of the Steens, when the stock was being changed to Hereford from the roan that prevailed in the 90s. Note how the snow is still holding on the top of that more than 9,000-foot range.

Above: Looking up at the Steens from a dry lake bed at its eastern base. Elevation of the peak is 9,354 feet, and it is more than 5,000 feet above the lake bed. *Below:* Looking down from the Steens and eastward toward the far-flung expanses of Alvord Desert, which, itself, is 4,000 feet above sea level. This view is on the opposite side of the range from the Malheur Refuge.

To a true cowman, a cow is a sort of fellow creature that must be carefully tended, provided with proper food and water, and cared for in sickness. When she is sold, the cowman follows her up the ramp to the freight car with a touch of guilt in his heart; for mere pelf he is parting with something he liked and respected. Such a cowman was Peter French.

PETER FRENCH

HUGH JAMES GLENN

Above: John William "Peter" French, most famous of the western cattlemen, controlled a 200,000-acre range empire in the Donner und Blitzen Valley of Southeast Oregon, when, in 1897, a bullet fired by an irate settler ended his meteoric career. This is his only known photograph.

Below: Dr. Hugh James Glenn, partner and financial backer of Peter French, was recognized Wheat King of the western world when, in 1883, he was shot to death by an angry bookkeeper. His daughter Ella, Peter's wife, presented this photograph to the Willows Library in California.

Cowboys bringing in the cows and calves for branding in the Peter French Country of Southeastern Oregon. Roping and branding is still done on the open range here much as it was in the days when French ran the P Ranch.

Al Monner

Almost a century ago, French set a pattern for modern cow ranches, with emphasis on improving both the land and the cattle by the best scientific methods available.

Horse corral fence made of stout juniper posts, similar to many of the fences that French constructed.

A lofty view of the P Ranch taken before 1898, showing the brush corrals and the long horse barn, which still stands. The white house is hidden among the poplars beyond the barn at the left.

Al Monner

Old feed rack for cattle—built entirely of juniper posts.

Close-up of the long horse barn which Peter French built from hewn aspen and juniper timbers about 1880. It is still in excellent condition, except for some lost shingles. Note how straight the ridgepole has remained.

H. H. Sheldon

Interior of the long barn, showing the solid construction of the framework.

Peter French sent freight teams like this south to Surprise Valley, and north to the Blue Mountains, to haul supplies back to his ranches. These trips had to be made during the summer, and the load limited to but a few tons.

Close-up of a freight wagon dating from the pioneer days of the Steens Mountain country, when they were the only means of getting supplies into that remote region.

An early picture of the round barn on the P Ranch, but it looks much the same today. The entrance to the left led directly into the stone corral in the center, and was presumably the only entrance used when French's vaqueros were breaking horses there.

Two views of French's beef wheel, near the long barn. The wheel is still occasionally used. Animal carcasses were hauled up by the gambrel—seen hanging from the rope at the end of the shaft. The shaft was then turned by a rope on the square frame. If French learned that a family was short of meat in the winter, he would send half a beef over to them—but more often the settler took care of that problem himself.

Interior view of the round barn, with a close-up of the center post, showing the construction of the braces that hold the middle section.

This photograph of Fort (Camp) Harney was taken in 1872, the year that Peter French first rode into the Harney Basin. Just six years later, settlers fled here to escape from the Paiutes and Bannocks, who were raiding ranches, killing and burning. French earlier purchased the sawmill that A. H. Robie had used to make the lumber for the camp buildings.

Winnemucca, Nevada, in 1868, a few years before French began driving his cattle to its markets.

French set out for Oregon in June of 1872, driving up the Sacramento River with twelve hundred head of cattle, half a dozen Mexican vaqueros, and a Chinese cook. He probably crossed the river at Red Bluff, because he knew the road to that place and the capacity of the ferry. He also knew something about the trail that led to Shingletown, and that he was sure to be able to find the directions to Lost Camp, north of Mount Lassen, and on to Susanville—if he decided to go that far before turning north to Fort Bidwell. The road had been well traveled. Packers had moved over it with supplies for the Idaho mines, a few years before, when Red Bluff was competing with The Dalles in Oregon, as a shipping point for supplies to the mines in Eastern Oregon and Idaho territory. There thousands of miners dug gold and silver so intently they did not take time to hunt; and so profitably they were glad to pay high prices for food and clothing.

Stockmen had also driven cattle over the route. In 1865, Major G. G. Kimball trailed three thousand head of sheep over the road, taking along a wagon to haul equipment and supplies. This was the northern route, which was considered an easier trail than the one running south of Mount Lassen. It would have been possible to turn northward a few miles out of Lost Camp, but that trail was along ridges. Because cattle move slowly and need water frequently, French probably went as far as Fredonia, near Susanville, before heading toward Fort Bidwell.

He could have crossed the Sacramento at Chico and gone up Butte Creek by Lake Almanor, but in any case he would have gone

41

by Fort Bidwell in Surprise Valley, where there was a trading post. From the lush feed in this valley, he shoved his band of young and vigorous cows over a low pass into Warner Valley. There the feed around the lakes was high and rich.

The young cattleman then turned east to cross the numerous dry lake beds of that region, and pass by Beatys Butte on the south. He next traversed present Catlow Valley, a wide and dry area that little fits the description of a valley. Traveling northeast, he approached the range of hills bordering the Blitzen Valley on the west, camping near some springs to let his cattle rest and feed after their long passage through the dry country.

There at the springs, Peter French had a visitor by the name of Porter, who was attracted by the smoke of a strange fire. Porter's main interest was in prospecting, though he had a few head of cattle he herded while looking for gold. But his luck had been poor and he was discouraged. He had decided he was never going to find gold in the Blitzen Valley, or in the mountains around it. He even warned French against bringing so many cattle into the country, explaining that they might attract roving bands of Indians; the big meadow in the Blitzen Valley could be a trap for untended cattle. During the meeting, the lonesome, disheartened Porter gladly sold his small band of a dozen or so cows to French, who paid for them with money supplied by Dr. Glenn. The purchase included a branding iron giving Peter French ownership of all cattle in the valley wearing a "P" on their left hip.

Porter's cattle ran between Roaring Springs and the valley of the upper Blitzen. The fact that there was no other brand on that range made the land technically his, under the existing rules of possession. "First come, first served" decided the range rights of much of the West in the days of the big spreads. If a man moved into a territory and used the grass, he was entitled to continue using it and to expand until he came to the border of another cattleman's range. Usage, rather than outright ownership of the land itself, determined the right to control — but grass was all a cattleman wanted anyway.

In 1872, land was not considered valuable; grass was the important asset, and then only when used in the year it grew. If a steer ate the grass and waxed fat and was sold and butchered to feed hungry people, a service was performed jointly by grass and steer and man. Ownership of the land made no difference.

Few white men had been in this valley. Men under Peter Skene Ogden trapped out the beaver prior to 1830. Major Enoch Steen, who gave his name to the mountain, headed a party that left The Dalles in 1860 to find a route for a wagon road from that outpost to Salt Lake City. He was under orders from General William S. Harney, who was eager to improve transportation in Oregon. Harney thought there should be a better route than the one down the John Day Valley, for miners on their way to Idaho.

The Donner und Blitzen River was named by Colonel George B. Currey, who crossed it in 1864, during a foray against the Snakes. It was storming that day, and the little river was high and boiling at Rock Ford—the only spot with bottom solid enough for a ford. With lightning flashing and thunder rolling, the well-read colonel remembered his German lessons and named the river the *Dunder und Blitzen*—now the Donner und Blitzen, or sometimes just the Blitzen.

Although the valley of the lower Donner und Blitzen River was to become known as the best cattle range in Southeastern Oregon, it had not been pre-empted by the first cattlemen who came into the country. John Devine started his White Horse Ranch east and south of the Steens, where four small creeks made a small oasis. Peter Stenger and two other men had built the Sod House in 1872, but did not penetrate into the Blitzen Valley. A reason for this appears in the *Monthly Weather Review,* May 1937, where F. P. Kean projected precipitation for this part of Oregon by tree rings. He showed that, from 1854 to 1869, there was a wet season with a cumulative increase in precipitation of 111 per cent. This amount of additional moisture in so wet a place as the Blitzen Valley could have been the reason that earlier stockmen kept their stock out of it. They were afraid to let their untended cattle near the swampy valley; besides, there was lots of land elsewhere. So, the Blitzen Valley was left for Peter French.

From their camp in the upper Blitzen Valley, young French and his Mexican vaqueros could look north and east to the range land on the west side of the river, south of present Frenchglen. This land rises to a ridge some 6,100 feet high, with a steep west slope, to the Catlow Valley, into which Home Creek, Dry Creek, and Kuney and Black canyons drain. Water from these is quickly absorbed in the flat of the Catlow Valley, except in the wettest years and in the wettest places, such as Roaring Springs. There water makes a meadow of the valley floor. East of the ridge, the waters drain into the Blitzen. This whole country is good cattle range, not so luscious nor so permanently green as the flat valley of the lower Blitzen, but it produces strong, succulent bunchgrass.

Eastward the fifty-mile-long Steens rises 9,354 feet, to cast a shadow far onto the Alvord Desert. Fourteen creeks and rivers carry its snow waters to the Donner und Blitzen River. Indian Creek, McCoy Creek, the little Blitzen, and the deep gash in the earth that is Kiger Gorge, make definite breaks in the west slope of the Steens, and carry most of the water. All this is fine cattle range. Stock can start from the bottom in the spring and work their way to the top, finding, till late summer, fresh grass that has been watered by long-lying snow.

The Blitzen comes into the flat lands from the Southeast, where, beaten white by the rocks, it drops four thousand feet in less than twenty-five miles. Once on the valley floor, the river quietly picks up its tributaries while ambling sedately into shallow Malheur Lake. To hem in this valley, which is thirty miles long and five miles wide, the Jackass Mountains rise on the west, giving some protection from that direction.

The rugged Steens and the Blitzen Valley are but the southern part of the vast Harney Basin that drains into Malheur Lake. The northern part of it is larger by half. That part is watered from the Blue Mountains. Numerous creeks and the Silvies River (named for Antoine Sylvaille) flow from the Blues. Like the Blitzen to the south, when the Silvies River reaches the valley floor near Burns, it slows down and grudgingly makes its way to shallow Malheur Lake, as if reluctant to mix its pure, mountain water with that of the brackish, tule-grown, muddy lake. Here the river divides, the west branch running close to Wright's Point, a stray bit of hill that partially divides the Harney Basin. The east branch reaches the lake in a different place. Between the two branches is what has long been called the Island Ranch, almost as famous for cattle production as the Blitzen.

Most of the water that drains through the flat lands from both north and south comes to Malheur Lake, a body of alkali-impregnated water that once covered forty thousand acres, no part of which exceeded five feet in depth. Dry seasons rapidly reduce the lake; evaporation takes a toll of forty inches a year, and irrigation prevents the lake from receiving its normal amount of water. The lake varies greatly in size from the spring run-off until fall. Once, in a different geographical and geological time, Malheur Lake drained south and east into the south fork of the Malheur River, that flows to the Snake. Now the lake is a dead sea with no outlet.

Except for a few springs and springtime creeks, no water enters Harney Lake except that from Silver Creek, which flows from the Blue Mountains west of Burns. The fluctuating size of the lakes causes a large body of shore land useful for winter grazing. Then, thousands of acres are exposed long enough to produce a grass suitable for cattle.

The Harney Basin is thus watered by streams from two mountain ranges whose waters meet in a shallow lake. The basin is roughly seventy-five miles long and from twenty to forty miles wide. It contains two major rivers and numerous creeks with fertile bottoms, as well as some deep gorges where snow stays until late summer to keep the streams running. There are broad ranges and meadows where thousands of cattle can feed throughout a long summer in the comfort that causes calves to grow and cows to stay fat. As the autumn snows drive the cattle to lower levels, there are the valleys of the Blitzen and the Silvies, where snow seldom lies long and where the grass grows tall and thick.

Grant County — in which Steens Mountain, the Donner und Blitzen River, and the whole Harney Basin were located in the 1870s—was established in 1864, after the discovery of gold on Canyon Creek. When the great influx of miners arrived, the seat of huge Wasco County at The Dalles seemed a long way off for the modest functions provided by, or required from, county government. As a result, residents obtained separation from Wasco County and took the name of Grant, a timely name to choose in 1864. By 1870, there were but 2,251 persons in Grant County's 14,664 square miles, and most of these were searching for gold along the John Day River or at the Austin gold camp; or they were soldiers at Fort Harney. There were no incorporated cities, no settled establishments, no stores selling anything but tools and essentials, and only meager signs of government.

Not until 1889 was Harney County carved from Grant, with Burns becoming the county seat one year later.

WHEN PETER FRENCH LOOKED DOWN ON THE valley of the Blitzen in the summer of 1872, it was green with high grass and dry enough in most places for his cattle to pasture safely. The swamp worried him less than it did his contemporaries, for he intended to watch his stock carefully. There was to be no wandering, untended, into treacherous areas. Dr. Glenn had trusted him and given him a chance; and Peter French was determined to do his part as well as he could. There would be no turning of cattle loose on a wide range, however good, letting them rustle for themselves. Neither would they be lost in swamps. Peter French intended to be a cattleman in a more modern style than others in the West, who, from Montana to Texas, let cattle run the range untended.

This valley, surrounded by sloping hills on which grass grew as high as a man's stirrups, looked like cattle heaven to Peter French, and he thought it could be just that if range and cattle were properly managed. Even now, the valley looks that way, and certainly no cowman has stood on the rim of Jackass Mountain, above the old P Ranch, without breaking the commandment, "Thou shalt not covet."

French intended to own that valley, all of it, bottom and hill—whether from ambition or avarice, from loyalty to Dr. Glenn or from simple ego. He wanted it, and he got it.

Near the spot where the Blitzen reaches the bottom, French set up headquarters. Here in an entirely strange land, he had no more than half a dozen men to look after his band of cattle and construct some necessary buildings. Though it was summer and the days warm with sunshine, still it was time to get ready for winter, the intensity of which he could not estimate.

He learned that at Fort Harney, seventy miles to the north, there was a small sawmill owned by Albert H. Robie, who, in 1867, had brought the machinery from Boise to saw lumber for the interior of the fort. From this mill French obtained lumber to build a house to shelter his men and to give his Chinese cook, Charley On Long, a feeling of greater security.

Robie's team of sixteen oxen brought the first lumber, but in a short time French had broken horses to make up his own freight team. He cut poles and brush for corrals, weaving the willows through the posts for some; using shorter erect willows for others. Such corrals will last a lifetime with little repair. From Fort Bidwell he obtained a mower and rake to put up some hay for the stock, in preparation for winter.

French and his little crew had the valley to themselves—lost in a wealth of space and busy building a cow ranch. By 1873, he was sending eight- and ten-horse freight teams to Surprise Valley in California, and as far north as La Grande, to obtain tools, harness, nails, glass, machinery, and saddles. The teams also brought back tons of wire for fencing. French made a reputation in Harney County for the quality of his fences and the miles of it he built. The wire was smooth, without the barbs that were first added to fence wire in 1874, though not successfully till 1877. The wagons also brought salt and sugar, soda for sour dough, coffee, beans and flour.

Peter French set out an orchard near his house, planting it with apples, plums, crab apples, gooseberries, and even some of the softer fruits. Red June apples may still be picked from the trees he planted. His bottom land produced garden vegetables of the more durable varieties, even though the elevation was more than four thousand feet. A garden could not be grown here as early as in lower altitudes, but root crops and the hardier vegetables could be had by dropping the seed and keeping the cows out of the patch. There were trout in the river right at the door; deer hid in the clumps of willows near the house; antelope sped through the sage, and bighorn sheep could still be found. Grouse and ducks lived in this valley that is now a refuge for all kinds of birds.

Sometimes Peter kept hogs for bacon and ham, though he usually purchased these. The staple foods—and there was no other kind—all came by wagon. Though there were no luxuries, neither was there hunger. The men at the P Ranch had good food. French saw to that. The big beef wheel near the barn was used as often as needed to provide the meat. A beef wheel raised a beef carcass into the air for dressing and was high enough to take it beyond the reach of dogs or coyotes.

Ranch hands had few diversions—maybe a little music by banjo, mouth organ, or jew's-harp, when time and mood permitted. There was little to read, though French was a subscriber to the Colusa *Sun.* There was always a jug of liquor for medicinal purposes, and women were a sometime thing.

These first years in Oregon set the pattern for the future success of the P Ranch. During that time, French and his Mexicans came to know the country—the wet spots in the meadow where cattle could be lost, the richest grass slopes along the west side of the Steens, the time to calve, and the time to bring the cattle down from the hills before the winter snows. This is the sort of knowledge, part of it intuitive, a stockman must have if he is to prosper.

The crew that rode up from California was large enough for a start, where range was open and plentiful, and where there was no one, except wandering Indians, to steal stock or supplies. The Mexicans stayed year after year, liking the location and their boss more and more.

A list of men working at the P Ranch shows the Mexican names of Vincenti Ortego, Juan Ortego (who homesteaded the P Ranch quarter section and sold it to French in 1882), Juan Charris, Jesus Charris, Prim "Tebo" Ortego, Joquim "Chino" Berdugo—often the range boss—and Francisco "Chico" Chararataguey. Some of them sent for their relatives. As time went on and the crew expanded, American names appeared.

In those days, it was not at all unusual for a young man to saddle his horse some bright morning, tie a few blankets behind the cantle, pocket some food, and go out to make his own way. Even if he were still in his teens, no sheriff was put on his trail, and no tears were shed at his assumption of manhood. A young man, or an old one, could find food and shelter at any big cow ranch—and perhaps a job. He had to work wherever he was—and life was not easy anywhere.

Men on the P Ranch worked hard because there was nothing else to do. Besides, it was what they came for. It went on winter and summer because Peter French was a good boss, who somewhere had learned that the way to keep a crew satisfied was to keep them busy—they quarrel less and stay longer, when occupied. In a way, the P Ranch was a monarchy; everyone knew who was to give the orders. French told the men when to start, what to do—and how, if necessary. Workingmen expected this and respected a man who could keep the details of a large ranch in mind and ramrod its operations. The P Ranch boss took the lead, speaking in quiet tones but with authority. When he said, "Tebo, take these two men and ride out the little Blitzen," that is what was done.

Stockmen kept order in the Old West; riders from a well-disciplined outfit seldom got into trouble. The nearest law from the Blitzen was a hundred and fifty miles away at Canyon City. This put discipline in the hands of the ranch boss, who held the economic and social power to guide the community, aided by his own personal prestige and respect.

Wages for experienced cow hands were $30 to $35 a month, slightly less for beginners. Foremen earned up to $60 or $65 and "found," meaning the employe could spread his blankets on a shelf in the bunkhouse and have a place at table when at headquarters.

On the range working cattle, the rider laid his blankets on some form-fitting spot of ground and ate from a plate on his lap.

As the French spread grew, it became necessary to keep certain supplies in stock at the ranch for the benefit of the men. When a rider's boots gave out or he tore his pants, he needed replacements. Chewing and smoking tobacco were essential. According to ranch records, "Old Yank" Langley had to have his chewing tobacco even if it did cost twenty-five cents a plug. Chewing tobacco was Peter French's only indulgence in the sins of unnecessary consumption.

By 1877, the P Ranch store was doing business with settlers as well as employes. John Devine contracted a debt of $20 on one trip to the Blitzen Valley. Ed Kiger bought a saddle for $37. Store records show sales of items not essential to the cow business, such as the sale of a suit of clothes to Frank Chapman for $24 and of a watch and ring to John South for $33.75. Probably these last items were bought elsewhere and charged on the company books, for a man known to be working for a big cow outfit had credit wherever he might be.

Evidence of the growth of the P Ranch shows in the size of the figures in French's long account journals. French himself entered some items, while others were written by employes detailed to look after the store and accounts—perhaps because of illness or broken bones, or some other ailment or condition that barred them from the jobs of cattle herding, fence repairing, ditch digging, or horse breaking. Sometimes a record of thousands of dollars received from the sale of cattle will be followed on the next line by an entry concerning the sale of tobacco to a rider.

Withdrawals of money for French's use and payments to Glenn appear on the same page and with no greater emphasis than a man's wages. It must be assumed that these notations were the daily record, the background for all business transacted. That is the basis on which all bookkeeping is done and it is what French did— and all he did. To pay off a man, he merely referred to the last settlement, figured the time, and deducted his withdrawals and purchases. To know how much to send to Dr. Glenn required only the addition of receipts and the deduction of ranch expenses.

A great deal of money was paid to Glenn and a good many dollars were received from him. To reach a balance in this late day would be a job for an expert accountant, aided by a talented mind reader.

French gave his personal note to many men, probably for the purchase of land; some amounts are too large for cattle deals only. The doctor knew that French was going to buy all the land he could and that he, Glenn, was going to furnish the money for it— if P Ranch earnings were insufficient. On his part, French knew that his deals would be backed by Glenn, who never came to Oregon to check on the progress of the ranch. If French gave his note for land, he was sure to be repaid in time; and he could always use the receipts from the sale of cattle to buy more land.

Since there was no bank near this growing community of southern Grant County, French kept a supply of cash at the ranch, although not enough for the hundreds of transactions he handled. Many deals were made by the circulation of notes from men whose signature on a piece of paper was good enough to be negotiable. A $20 note was as good as a $20 gold piece, if there were confidence in the financial and moral integrity of the signer. Notes were endorsed by simple signatures. Since they were not signed "without recourse," each signer was liable for payment. Such paper circulated freely, checks as well as notes serving as currency or gold.

French gave S. B. Kiger his note for $1,710 with interest at one per cent a month, a customary rate for short-term paper, although money could sometimes be borrowed for ten per cent a year. He paid P. Bohn $500 in cash and gave his note for $4,400 on the ranch. Checks and commercial paper are used for cash even in these days, but in the seventies in Grant County, it was necessary to use any evidence of indebtedness as a circulating medium.

By 1877, the owner of the P Ranch was getting acquainted in Canyon City, the county seat of Grant County. In November of that year, he wrote: Expenses Canyon City $60; by lawyer fee $11; by mdse. (merchandise) $22.37; bought serif (sheriff) order $725. Gave gold coin for same $548.25 (French apparently bought some land from the sheriff at a reduced price). On the same trip he left $1,000 for Osborn and bought a pair of boots for $14.

Whatever was needed in the way of services was done on the ranch; everyone did his own work. Winter was the time for a rider to get his equipment in repair for the longer days of summer. The men spent winter evenings putting new stirrup leathers on saddles, braiding ropes out of rawhide, repairing harness and sewing patches on clothes, for every man was his own seamstress.

Clothes were really not much of a problem; they were simple and utilitarian. Peter French's men dressed like other western cowmen. Their pants were of loose-fitting denim or wool; their shirts of some durable material of neutral color — especially after a few washings in cold water and lye soap. Shirts were not silk, nor any imitation thereof. If a man liked a touch of color he might wear a bright-colored neckerchief, perhaps a silk one. A neckerchief was a useful article of wear. It could keep dust from falling down the neck, or be pulled up to shield the mouth and nose when driven cattle kicked up a thick dust.

Boots were heavy cowhide. Often rough and ill-fitting, they made heavy wool or cotton sox desirable. Vests were common because they are the most useful garment a man in the open can wear. When unbuttoned, they hang loosely without binding; when buttoned, they are snug and warm. Besides, they have pockets in which to carry matches—the old sulphur kind that came in bunches —along with tobacco, a few nails, and maybe a bit of jerky. The vest was a portable roll-top desk.

Hats were generally of wool and large enough from which to water a horse. A wide-brimmed hat could be tied down around the ears with a handkerchief, to keep them from freezing in a blizzard. Underwear was long and usually woolen, the most comfortable kind for men who live outdoors. Records of the sale of woolen winter overcoats are common in the French journals. Sheepskin and insulated coats were unknown in the seventies and eighties. Men wore chaps the year around, heavier ones in winter for warmth and lighter ones in summer for protection from brush. Some said they were cool in summer because the wind blew up them.

A man going out to look after cattle probably took along a hammer, or better yet, a pair of heavy pliers so he could get through fences and also repair broken ones. A few staples came in handy.

When riding to look after cattle, a man often packed a rifle because of coyotes, wolves, bobcats, and other predators that killed calves and destroyed game. The television concept of a cowman strapping on a six-gun at the start of a day's work is modern and fictitious. A carbine in a saddle sheath was a better weapon for coyotes—and did much less banging around. A revolver was a poor tool for anything but close work, although it did make a fearful and impressive noise.

Even in usually dry Southeastern Oregon, a slicker tied behind the saddle was sometimes found useful before night; and a man, going out on the range for a day, first went by the cookhouse to get a couple of biscuits to put in his chap pockets. It might grow dark before he could eat again.

THE FIRST CATTLE IN EASTERN OREGON WERE
driven up from Texas by drovers who saw a chance to make a
profit buying stock in the south and trailing them to the bunchgrass of Oregon, where they invariably grew and fattened better
than in Texas. Some stock had been brought across the Cascade
Mountains by men from the Willamette Valley, who owned descendants of the herds trailed up from California by Ewing Young.
However, these cattle were in the minority in Grant County. The
Californians who came to Oregon usually brought cattle from their
home state or from Nevada to start their herds, which meant that
there were eventually a good many California cattle in the Steens
Mountain country.

But, whether they were improved Texas cattle or imports from
California, Oregon cattle were generally desired by stockmen east
of the Rocky Mountains, because of their superior size and fleshing.
They were called American cattle, though Texas was certainly as
much a part of the United States as Oregon—but popular appella-
tions are not always factual.

Drives were organized in Oregon from as far west as Oregon
City, in the Willamette Valley, to cross the mountains near Mt. Hood
and strike east on a journey of more than a thousand miles, taking
an entire summer before the drovers could return home. During the
1870s—before the construction of the Oregon Short Line from Salt
Lake City to Portland—many thousand head of American cattle
were driven east by established dealers who went around buying
whole herds to send on the long trail to the grassy prairies, from

which the buffalo hunters and the Indians had so recently removed the native bison. Lang & Ryan, cattle dealers with headquarters in Kansas City and Omaha, were among the larger companies engaged in this business. It was reported that 60,000 head were sent east in 1878 and 100,000 in 1879.

Montana and Wyoming cattlemen bought Oregon cattle to improve their own herds. Even after the heyday of the big midwestern cattlemen, when homesteaders came to the great plains, the drives continued for the same reason. Railroad crews were hungry for beef, and the Federal government was usually obligated to feed Indians after they were sent to reservations. Cattle that had been down to $18 a head in the depression of the early seventies went to $25 and $30 in the early eighties. These higher prices helped build the financial sinews of the cattlemen in and around the Steens Mountain country.

P RANCH CATTLE

By the mid-seventies, the P Ranch had begun to earn some substantial income. The growth of cattle was good, there were few losses, and steers larger than the normal size were ready to be sold. This was the reputation of the French-Glenn spread for thirty years —good cattle. There were sound reasons for this.

Cows that Peter French brought up to Oregon were a select group of Shorthorn breeding, and he immediately started to buy good bulls, usually Shorthorn, as they were the most popular cattle in the West. These bulls were red and roan and occasionally white. They soon smoothed out the bony frame of native Texas cattle and shortened the horns. After a couple of crosses, longhorns ceased to be the running gear for a set of horns, becoming instead a rounded half ton of beef. Henry Miller, the butcher, astounded at the quality of French's cattle, once said: "These are the finest steers I ever saw."

The first record of a cattle sale from the P Ranch was on January 18, 1875, when French realized $7,157, almost two and a half years after he started the venture and after Glenn had put thousands of dollars into the operation for land, equipment, cattle, buildings, and general expense. This sale likely did not include steers raised from the cows brought up from California, since steers under three years old, preferably four, were usually not sold.

DRIVE TO WINNEMUCCA

When he began to drive cattle to market, Peter French bought the steers of smaller ranchers who could not profitably make the long drive to Winnemucca, Nevada, two hundred miles away. P Ranch accounts are full of items dealing with these transactions, apparently handled with complete confidence on both sides.

Peter French set the date for the drive because he had the largest number of marketable cattle; he also furnished the crew for the drive. The time of the drive was late fall or winter because prices seemed best then. Besides, it was the end of the grass year, and moisture from winter rains made it easier to move cattle over the rather barren country between the Blitzen Valley and Winnemucca. With water along the route there was less danger of stampedes; such outbursts of bovine mob rule were dangerous and destructive.

Men who had steers to market could either sell them to French outright or send them along on a sort of consignment basis. If the latter, they depended on French to separate their steers from the others in the yards at Winnemucca and sell them to a buyer. In any case, some payment for the service of driving and selling would have been proper, if not always exacted.

When driving cattle through a cattle country, a crew picks up additional members—some more social minded than the average—who want to go along with the gang. Fat cattle being driven to market are moved as slowly and quietly as possible. Vaqueros would not unduly excite the bunch, nor would they seek out and drive back some visiting animal that insisted on going along. Likewise a drover might lose a few cattle that grew tired or footsore and straggled behind. In any case, it would be remarkable for a small crew to drive several hundred head of cattle more than two hundred miles through country where there were other cattle and arrive at journey's end with the same number and the identical ones they started with.

A drive across the mountains and valleys between the P Ranch and the railroad at Winnemucca took about three weeks, if time were allowed to let the steers feed along the way—which was the common practice. A cook wagon always went along and, in cold weather, another wagon to carry the bed rolls of the riders. If it was too cold they could sleep in the wagon, that is, men not on night herd duty.

In Winnemucca — which looked like a city compared to the P Ranch—the saddle-weary riders found more than a market for their stock. They encountered the pleasures of their daydreams. In Winnemucca, there were round tables covered with green baize, across which poker chips moved to the man with the most skill and the best luck. There were men with big mustaches and gaudy arm bands, who dispensed liquids that made a man feel strong as a bull in a few moments and remorseful and contrite in a few hours. There were doors decorated with red lights where professional women waited. It was all excitement, different from the daily routine; a time to laugh and be gay, a fiesta. A chance to drive a bunch of fat steers to the corrals near some sizable town was a fine trip for cowhands. The womanless P Ranch had no sights like bustling waitresses, no conviviality like a party of friends around a bar.

Back home after the long ride in the winter's cold, there would be the same work to do, work that started early each morning and lasted past the early dark. Riders had few chores to do at the home ranch; such things were for the cooks, a roustabout, or the newest man on the job. A wrangler arose at dawn and brought the horse herd into a corral. After breakfast the riders went out to pick their mounts for the day. Each one had a string of horses varying from eight to fifteen, depending on how many colts he was breaking.

Experienced and regular riders always had to break out a bunch of young horses.

The individual rider decided what horse he wanted to ride and roped him, the choice depending on the work to be done that day and the qualities of the horse. If he were to be branding, he would need a horse used to roping; if he were going to ride with other men, he could ride and train a half-broken horse; if he were going to patrol a section of the country alone, he could use an older horse, past its peak for hard work—and safer. He led his chosen mount to the rack where saddles were kept, or to where he had left his saddle along a fence. If he were doing hard riding, he would need another horse by noon.

After Peter French had been in Oregon a few years, he had as good a string of cow horses as existed anywhere. As with cattle, he bred the cow horses up until they were fitted to the job. Old-timers who rode them described the P Ranch saddle band as good-sized for cow horses, with fine life and both strength and durability. Purebred stallions gave the size and speed, and the native cayuse provided the endurance and orneriness. Many of them needed to be broken all over again every morning, when a little bucking was expected by range riders; in fact, a little bucking was the mark of a horse's readiness for the day's work. Normally a cayuse never pitched long, just a few jumps to see, perhaps, if the rider himself were ready for the day's work.

BRANDING

Branding was usually done on the range because not many corrals were available. That meant the gathering of a bunch of cattle from some previously specified area onto a reasonably level spot. Men held them there by constantly riding around them. Calves were roped and dragged to an open fire as soon as the branding irons were hot. With hind legs stretched out, the calf was branded, the mark of ownership being imprinted on the hide. The ears were cut in accordance with the ranch marking and the dewlap sliced from the skin under the neck. Young bulls became steers with a few deft strokes of a knife. Then the calf was free to run back to his bawling mother, held back by a protecting horseman.

French's brand was the "P" on the left hip for both horses and cattle; it was placed somewhat higher on the cattle. The ear mark was an under half crop on the left ear, meaning that about a quarter of the ear was cut off. The dewlap was cut upward. A dewlap cut downward was more likely to be lost. However, there were cattle with all kind of brands on the P Ranch, for French bought out many other stockmen and it was not customary to rebrand except on young cows that were to be kept for several years.

TENDING CATTLE

Looking after the cattle called for constant vigilance. They had to be on good grass and near water. There was some fear of predators, but there was not much rustling of cattle in the Steens Mountain country; it was too far from market for any thief. When settlers came in, they stole a certain amount of cattle, but on a retail basis, rather than wholesale.

A common practice of stockmen who had access to Malheur Lake was to put cattle around it when the water was low in winter and let them eat the grass that had grown during the summer. This was called "swamping." Cattle in such pasturage had to be watched carefully, for they would drown in a few inches of water if they mired down. Sometimes the lake froze over and cattle and horses would break through and be helpless.

In winter there was little feeding of cattle, though French always cut some hay in the event of a heavy snow, but snow was rare in the Blitzen Valley. He was the first Harney Basin stockman to provide hay for winter, partly because he had the best hay land and partly because it was his policy to be prepared. Hay was usually stacked, instead of being cut and raked into bunches as it is today. Modern farmers use machinery for the entire operation, whereas eighty or ninety years ago haying was mostly hand labor. The hay was cut with a mower and raked into windrows, shocked for curing, and hauled by wagon to a stack. Modern machinery can bunch a ton of hay, making stacking unnecessary.

Success in the stock business, whether today, in the day of Peter French, or in Biblical times, depends on savvy. A cowman has to be able to tell, even at a distance, how a bunch of cattle is doing, whether the feed is sufficient, how the calves are growing, and if there is evidence of disease.

CATTLEMEN'S CONTRACTS

The usual arrangement between a man with cattle or sheep and another with a desire to manage and care for them was that the herder receive a third of the income and increase. Many men built fortunes, who began with nothing more than a willingness to care for stock. Owners seldom suffered from starting young men who could be depended on to stay with the animals and look out for them. Dr. Glenn made such an agreement with E. Waller Crutcher, who ran Glenn cattle a few years in Nevada. However, no agreement has been found between Peter French and Hugh Glenn. There are papers referring to a contract, but nothing said of its terms. At any rate, French did leave California with money and was never without it as long as Glenn lived. He did not get the usual third.

In other such contracts no real property was involved as it was assumed the stock would be run on public land. Ownership of land tied the old stockman down to a particular location, and a poor grass year might make it advisable to move. However, they did like to own the land around springs and to have a few acres for buildings and corrals.

The French-Glenn arrangement was different from most owner-herder partnerships because land was involved. French bought land because he thought it was valuable and believed others would buy it if he didn't. He himself took up a homestead and encouraged his men to take homesteads, which he bought; and he gained possession of land by any legal means available. French liked land as well as he did cattle, and the money he spent on it could account for the comparatively small percentage of the income he received from the partnership.

SWAMPLAND

Until well into the twentieth century, the policy of the Federal government was to get land into the hands of citizens. Before the Homestead Act was passed in 1862, the government recognized the rights of squatters, if they seemed to want to stay on the land they had pre-empted. The whole history of land acquisition by private citizens shows considerable sharp practice by them and much indecision on the part of the Federal government. Many ways were open to Americans who wanted to acquire some of the public domain—and sentiment was on their side.

One of the ways to obtain government land was peculiar to Grant County and other parts of Southeastern Oregon, where there was enough swamp or overflow land to arouse avarice. Shortly after Oregon became a state (1859), Congress passed a law providing that provisions of the Swamp Act be applicable to it, though the original act was written for the state of Arkansas, where conditions were far different from those of Southeastern Oregon. The law specified that within two years after the adjournment of the then-sitting legislature, Oregon was to describe its swamp land. Oregon failed to do so. In fact, the state did not even pass a law to implement the Swamp act until 1870. The result was several first-rate political scandals, most of them in Grant County.

A number of Oregon citizens took advantage of the state government's slowness to act, and some of them were in high positions. In the first report of applicants for swamp land, in 1872, were men who already were, or who became, public officials. They included a governor, a justice of the supreme court, a secretary of state, and a state treasurer, to say nothing of lesser officials. Some of the more practical ones began coming to the State Land Board with descriptions of land that they swore was swampy. They paid twenty per cent down for a title that was held valid by the courts. They agreed, of course, to drain the land in accordance with the law. Few did.

Oregon's record of public lands granted to it at the time of statehood seems inexcusable in retrospect. The state received 46,080 acres of university land; 500,000 acres of internal improvement land; 6,400 acres of capital building land; salt spring land up to 46,080 acres; 90,000 acres of agricultural, swamp and overflow land to be reclaimed, plus two sections of land in every township for common schools.

For years the state did nothing about it. The land was neither specifically claimed nor surveyed, nor was any evidence of ownership given to the Federal government. Rather, the state waited patiently until some prospective purchaser decided he would like to buy a parcel of land. Whereupon the state sold some to him, usually for one dollar per acre, eventually reporting the transaction to the Federal government. It was years before the state had obtained title to its quota of granted land, and only by the grace of the Federal government was it able to get all it had been granted.

"HEN" OWENS—PROMOTER

Until 1905, when President Theodore Roosevelt started prosecuting the promoters for land fraud, many men obtained public land illegally. The movement, though, was too late to catch those who got the swamp land. Most prominent among them was Henry C. Owens of Eugene City. He purchased thousands of acres of Oregon land for one dollar per acre, paying a fifth down—and the state often accepted his promise for that fifth. Owens bought for others, not having a desire to own the land himself.

The record does not show that any fortunes were made from Owens' deals; in fact, he hurt his clients more often than he did the state. He actually performed a service to the state by selling land for one dollar an acre in the seventies and eighties, that is even now worth little more than that. Clients thought they were cheating the state—a common bait for all suckers. Had the land not been sold, it would have remained in the hands of the Federal government until someone homesteaded it. Payment for the land obtained by Owens went to Oregon; without his manipulations, it would have remained Federal property.

"Hen" Owens made an affidavit to the state as to the swampy character of the land; this was accepted and made official. Whether he actually mounted a boat on a wagon and rode over thousands of acres of desert so he could honestly swear that he had been over it in a boat, has not been proved, but government laxity was such that the story is believable. The story, however, was not original in Oregon, having been told in other states before.

Owens was no small-time operator. On July 26, 1880, Certificate of Sale No. 123 was issued to him for 55,185.36 acres. In the biennium of 1880-1882, he purchased 67,326.32 additional acres, and, by 1884, he had acquired 228,867.99 acres. There was never that much swamp land in Oregon. W. D. Todhunter bought 34,859.42 acres, most of which later came into the ownership of Henry Miller. It was not until the late eighties, when settlers were trying to get land around Malheur Lake, that investigation was started to determine the legality of the swamp land purchases. Miller's Pacific Livestock Company won the first round, but in 1914, paid the state $125,000 and opened some land to settlement.

Citizens of Oregon have protested violently about the sale of land under the Swamp Act, saying that the school fund was robbed. Had the land actually been swampy, and held until it was developed, it would have been worth more; but land that was not swampy, though sold as such, was a clear gain to the state and the schools. The state really defrauded the Federal government through the connivance of "Hen" Owens.

French and Glenn did not have to resort to subterfuge or dishonesty to obtain land; they had money with which to buy it. All they needed was to find someone with a valid title to the land. Because they had control of the Blitzen Valley, no other stockman could use the big range on Steens Mountains without invasion of their rights. French has often been accused of buying land that was not swampy at the swamp land price. The charge is not correct. He did buy some swamp land, and did fence in land that didn't belong to him. Though later he had to take the fence down, he kept right on using the grass. The government got the land; French got the grass.

PAIUTE-BANNOCK REVOLT

DURING THE CIVIL WAR THE BLUE-CLAD UNION soldiers who guarded the West were recalled to fight the Southerners, and the job of defending the frontiers was left to local troops. Oregon was then a very young state, with small population, little money, and not much interest in fighting Indians. A small cadre of men had been left at Fort Vancouver, some troops had been sent up from California, and a few companies had been organized by the state government. But no one knew who was in charge. The result was confusion. Recruited local soldiers signed up for short enlistment periods of only ninety days, then left to mine gold in Eastern Oregon or Idaho—which was much more exciting, and occasionally more profitable, than chasing Indians.

The Paiute and Bannock tribes consequently did just about as they pleased during the Civil War years. They raided settlements, stole stock—especially horses—burned cabins, attacked pack or wagon trains and killed a number of white miners and settlers.

After the war the government dispatched General George Crook to Boise to stop this marauding. Crook had served his military apprenticeship in the West before the war. He liked Indians, had learned to talk some of their language, and understood their dissatisfaction with the government, which stemmed largely from insufficient food deliveries to the reservations, the restrictions of reservation life, and insistence that the braves learn to farm. Crook had been in Boise no more than a month before he started his forays against the natives. He preferred to fight Indians in the winter when—if they could be dislodged from their quarters and their food supply destroyed—they were easily defeated. Indians never had much in the way of reserve supplies.

By 1868, Crook had the Paiutes and Bannocks on reservations, leaving the country open to California stockmen who wanted to move into Southeastern Oregon.

Thanks to General Crook, Indians had been no problem to settlers in the Blitzen Valley or the Steens Mountain country. The Paiutes were on the Southeastern Oregon Malheur River Reservation (established in 1872), a parcel of bottom land lying in what is now Malheur and Harney counties, along the north fork of the Malheur River and Warm Springs Lake. As the reservation contained but a few acres of tillable land and the Indians had neither the skill nor desire to farm, they were fed by the Federal government, though issues of rations were not regular nor always ample.

Dependence of the Indians on the government robbed them of self-respect. Furthermore, they were held in little esteem by many of the whites.

The Indians were not entirely without encouragement. In 1877, Chief Joseph, over in the Wallowas, rebelled after the United States permitted white men to invade the country that had been set aside for the Nez Perce by what the chief considered a binding treaty. Young men of the tribe insisted on revolt, and they crossed the Snake River into Idaho, to start one of the longest and most successful retreats in the history of Indian warfare, though it ended with the defeat of the Nez Perce warriors at Big Hole, close to the northern border of Montana. The Sioux victory over General George A. Custer, in 1876, on the Little Big Horn, also gave hope to the western Indians.

How much communication existed among the various tribes on reservations is still unknown. Some historians believe that the Nez Perce, Paiutes, Bannocks and Yakimas together planned a general uprising to drive the white men out. Bill Hanley was among those convinced that the uprising of 1878 was to be a war for Indian liberation, with Sitting Bull the major plotter. The white defenders apparently thought so too, for they prepared to halt the Indians of Southeastern Oregon at the Columbia River, and thus prevent them from joining the Yakimas.

The Bannock and Paiute war began shortly after Buffalo Horn, chief of the Bannocks, went to Governor Mason Brayman in Boise to request more guns and ammunition for killing game, complaining that the government did not supply enough beef. Buffalo Horn had been of some service—or felt he had—in the pursuit of Chief Joseph, and Brayman may have considered his plea worthy on that account. In any event, the governor issued the requested supplies. Buffalo Horn then raided Payne's Ferry on the Snake River, where his men killed a white man and woman. From there he attacked other white men's camps before going on into Oregon to join the Paiutes on the Malheur River Reservation. The Paiutes were led by Egan (Ehegante), a member of the Cayuse tribe, who had become chief through marriage.

White men living in the area were unaware of this joining of forces—as were the military men at Fort Harney. A detachment of troops that had started to Boise, under Colonel Reuben F. Bernard, was hastily recalled to warn settlers that the tribes had consolidated and that they were to come to the fort for safety. Most of them did, but Peter French did not. He went right on about his business—either not warned or unwilling to stop his work.

A band of Paiutes, riding along the east side of the Steens, drove Green Crowley and his son, James, from their home. The Crowleys managed to reach the White Horse Ranch and the protection of its stone buildings. The frustrated Indians returned to the Crowley cabin and burned it, as well as the buildings on the Anderson ranch.

Among the settlers who reported to Fort Harney were George Smyth and his family, including a married son, John, and a son-in-law, Stilly Riddle. Restless about their stock and untended homes, George Smyth and his son rode the fifty miles to their homes in Happy Valley a few days later. There they found everything in good order. The stock was doing well and their homes were undisturbed. They decided to return to the fort the next day.

About daybreak they heard a noise outside. Peering from an upstairs window, they saw around fifty Indians in the yard, carrying brush and wood toward the house with the apparent intention of setting it afire. The Smyths fired on the Indians, who retreated to safe positions from which they returned the fire. Soon the warriors could be heard on a side of the house that had no windows; there they set a fire. The Smyths remained indoors, shooting whenever they could see an Indian; but shortly they were so choked by smoke, and blistered by heat, they had to open the front door to try to escape. The Indians were prepared. They shot at the white men, who fell back into the house, where they were burned to death. The Indians destroyed other houses in Happy Valley later that same day.

Peter French, with a crew of sixteen men, was at the Diamond Ranch that day of July 14, 1878, preparing to brand some calves. A new settler from the Willamette Valley, Sylvester (Coon) Smith, had come over to the Diamond from Happy Valley, eight or ten miles to the northeast, to borrow the running gears of a wagon. He intended to haul some poles to build corrals. He stayed overnight at the ranch and early the next morning headed home with his equipment. On approaching the rim at the top of the grade (where French had fenced the valley with stone walls between the rimrock), Coon Smith saw a party of twenty to twenty-five Indians beyond the big gate. Hastily cutting his tugs, he mounted his fastest horses and raced back to the Diamond Ranch.

The Indians had some difficulty with the big wooden gate, which was fastened shut by a long rod pushed into a hole in a cliff. Never before had they seen such a contrivance. It took them several minutes to open the gate and take up the chase. By that time, Smith had sufficient lead to beat them to the ranch buildings. He rode in shouting,

"Indians, Indians!" The cowmen were just getting saddled up for the day's work. French immediately ordered,

"Saddle up as quick as God will let you, and don't forget to catch a horse for the Chinaman. I'll hold them back awhile." John South was sent to the meadow to warn John "Ochoco" Witzel, an eighteen-year-old lad from the Ochoco Valley, who was holding the horse band a short distance away.

French then took the only rifle in camp and crawled onto a gate where he could get behind the big juniper gatepost for protection. From there he opened fire on the red invaders. He stopped them only for a few minutes. Before long the Indians climbed the rocky hill to get a better shot at him.

Meanwhile, riding as hard as they could, the crew turned at the bend of the hill, following McCoy Creek, on the way to the P Ranch. The Chinaman had never ridden a horse and fell off before he had gone far. He was hiding under a bridge when the Indians killed him. Coon Smith's horse was already tired, causing him to fall behind the fleeing vaqueros, but he saved his life by catching the horse the cook had lost.

When French jumped down from the gatepost to make his escape, the Indians were right behind him. He followed his crew up the east side of McCoy Creek to the trail crossing. At a break in the rimrock, French took his horse out of range, crawled behind a rock and proceeded to fire the remainder of his bullets at the Indians. He killed some of them and managed to hold all of them back until his men were well on their way. The only casualty in his crew, except the Chinaman, was young "Ochoco" Witzel, who was shot in the thigh by a bullet that killed his horse. Later that day the Paiutes killed Tom Dixon and a man named Harrison, who were fishing in the Blitzen River.

The little party of white men stopped at the P Ranch to consider the best course of action. Deciding that they lacked both men and ammunition enough to repel a large body of Indians, they headed toward Fort Harney, but not down the Blitzen, which they feared might be full of hostile Indians. Instead, they rode to the west of Jackass Mountains, in some very rough country, crossing the Sand

Reef near Harney Lake. The men reached the fort the next day. It was a long, hard trip for the wounded John Witzel, riding with a bullet wound in his hip.

French never did find out how many Indians he killed that day, but nothing he had done since coming to the Blitzen Valley so enhanced his reputation for bravery. At Fort Harney he joined the soldiers under Colonel Bernard, who was glad to get the support of so determined a man. French was made a scout and ordered to lead the civilian volunteers under the orders of Orlando (Rube) Robbins, chief of a scouting detachment that had joined the men stationed at the fort. Many settlers also served with the soldiers.

After raiding the Blitzen Valley, where they burned buildings and drove off horses, the band of Indians that had attacked the Diamond Ranch and killed the Smyths made their way leisurely to a camp on Silver Creek. There they set up their tepees on a willow-covered, rocky flat, where there was fuel to cook the white man's beef. There they were joined by the main body of Indians under Buffalo Horn and Egan, and there the scouts found them, a week after their depredations in the Blitzen Valley. The report to Bernard was that there were more than a thousand Indians in the camp, including several hundred warriors.

Colonel Bernard had four companies of cavalry, about 160 men, yet, despite the difference in numbers, he decided to attack. On the night of June 22, he moved his soldiers to a camp a few miles from Silver Creek. In the early light of Sunday, June 23, Peter French and the civilian volunteers, under Scout Robbins, crept toward the camp from a short distance up the creek. Colonel Bernard with his cavalry was below. At dawn they both struck, riding through the willows, upsetting tepees, and shooting and shouting to stampede the horses.

It was a surprise attack. As each group of attackers reached the end of the camp, the men wheeled about and returned. Soon the red warriors fled to the bluffs, caught horses, and began a counter attack. Rube Robbins and Chief Egan engaged in a duel in which

Egan received a wrist wound and Robbins had his horse shot from under him. Peter French quickly rode over to Robbins, helped him mount behind his own saddle, and escape from the battle. Buffalo Horn was killed, along with nearly fifty of his braves. The troops lost four men.

Both sides claimed victory, but the losses of the Indians were much greater. After the battle, they fled north up Silver Creek, toward the Blue Mountains. Crossing the John Day River below Canyon City, they worked on toward Pendleton and Heppner, where residents threw up makeshift forts for protection, certain that the Indians were on their way to join the Yakimas. All available river boats were commandeered to patrol the Columbia River to prevent the Indians from crossing, should they attempt it.

The Indian attack faded. Near Ukiah, the Paiutes and Bannocks met some Umatillas, who betrayed Egan and killed him, delivering his head to an army officer in a sack. Without leadership, the red men, hungry, beaten, and discouraged, started back to their reservations. Soon the Federal government moved them to other reservations in distant states, breaking up the tribes in the process. The agency at Malheur Indian Reservation was abandoned and sold.

Long freight team in front of the pioneer Winnemucca Hotel in the 1880s, showing the Rhinehart store behind the wagons and the courthouse in the distance. A cattle drive here from the P Ranch took about three weeks, but the vaqueros welcomed the 200-mile ride because of the excitement they found in the old town—far different from their daily routine.

In 1889, Burns was a small community, with its lone hotel able to care for only two or three visitors and its stores stocked with little more than the necessities of life.

Hunting was once unrestrained east of the Cascades, and men lived on the plentiful wild meat produced by the native animals and birds.

Al Monner

This cabin in the Harney Basin was once the dwelling of a homesteader who tried to eke out a living on a barren slope in a semiarid land—where it sometimes takes thousands of acres for success.

Right: Buffalo Horn, Chief of the Bannocks, who triggered the Bannock-Paiute War in Southeast Oregon. *Left:* Typical regalia of a Bannock chief. *Below:* Members of a Bannock Indian camp, decked out in all their finery. Note the ever-present dog in the foreground.

The first building erected in Fields in Harney County. Note the carefully rounded fireplace.

Some Harney County pioneers of the 1870s, most of whom had a part in the history of the Blitzen Valley. Back row, from left: Tom Vickers, Mart Brenton, John Witzel, Chino Berdugo, Prim Ortego, Bill King. Front row: W. D. (Doc) Kiger, Stilly Riddle, Rye Smyth and wife, Nell, George Miller.

The Burns Hotel, built in 1892 on the corner of Broadway and A streets, across from Mart Brenton's Red Front Livery Stable and Trish & Donegan's Saloon. Here, it was said, Peter French and Ed Oliver quarreled at the Democratic convention in 1896, just about one year before French met death at the hands of Oliver.

The case of French-Glenn vs. Springer and the murder trial of Ed Oliver were both held in this old wooden courthouse in Harney County, built in 1894.

Roping calves for branding on the OO Ranch.

At Roaring Springs Ranch, in Catlow Valley, horses get their morning drink from the cool water of the springs for which the ranch is named. The springs burst from under the rimrock above the ranch buildings and rush noisily over the rocky slope until the water reaches the valley floor.

Alvord Ranch, situated at the base of Steens Mountain's highest ridges, became famous as a showplace under the ownership of John Devine, in the 1880s. He kept a stable of fine horses, herds of show cattle, and made the ranch a refuge for the wild animals and birds which lived there.

Devine's great barn still stands as a monument to the days when he made it the home for a great string of blooded race horses.

OLD SOD HOUSE RANCH

The old Sod House overlooking Sodhouse Springs, with Malheur Lake in the background. This ranch was the scene of Peter French's murder, almost three-quarters of a century ago.

➤

PETER FRENCH (FAR RIGHT) AND HIS P RANCH VAQUEROS

The Boss of the Blitzen had just delivered 2,100 steers to Wallula Junction in 1885, when he and his vaqueros lined up for this picture. Left to right: Burt French, Peter's brother; Charles Wheeler; Jim Brannon; Jack Cooper; Phil Burnhardy, the cook; Charles Ward; Kid Hudson; Bill Dyer; Mart Brenton; Abe Hostetter; Johnny Fisher; Boland Fine, and French.

MART BRENTON

DAVE CROW

Mart Brenton, in 1883, when he was working for the P Ranch. He is the buckaroo who claimed credit for kicking away the sand that allowed Malheur Lake to flow into Harney.

Dave Crow, who rode from the sagebrush field to Winnemucca, to carry news of Peter French's murder. Dressed here in his wedding suit, he gives little evidence of the physical hardiness that allowed him to ride two hundred miles through short, winter days without rest.

Ears up, manes flying, the horse herd comes racing in from the sage-covered range, driven by a pair of riders covered with the alkali dust of the upland.

P Ranch vaqueros—Billy Gilham, Chico, and Dave Crow—riding three horses they were breaking.

This deserted homestead east of Burns, Oregon, is typical of many others; its fallen and broken windmill a poignant reminder of the settlers' desperate need for water to cultivate an arid land.

Roping is an art and a forgotten one. The unseen roper has the front legs while the man in view of the camera has his big loop ready for the head. The scared colt is in for a new experience.

The famous white house on the P Ranch—Peter French's headquarters where he kept his books on engineering and his tracts on cattle raising—and where he entertained visiting cattlemen and cattle buyers, who were glad to be invited to the home of the Boss of the Blitzen. *Inset:* A picture taken during the fire which destroyed the white house, burning it to the ground and destroying many of the poplars surrounding it. Only one tall chimney still stands.

Frenchglen has survived the changes in cattle ranching because it is the last step from civilization for those hardy hunters and fishermen who want to visit the high Steens Mountain country. Sixty miles of gravel and paved roads link Frenchglen with Burns, Oregon. The cluster of buildings also marks the southern end of the great Malheur Wildlife Refuge.

The Frenchglen Hotel was built about 1916, as a stopping place for teamsters, who were needed to help the freight teams get up the hill to Catlow Valley, on their way to Winnemucca. Now its guest rooms are occupied by fishermen, photographers, bird watchers, and those who come to bask in the romance of a one-time cattle empire.

FRENCH-GLENN COMPANY

THOUGH THE INDIANS' REVOLT LASTED ONLY A FEW weeks, they caused considerable damage in the Harney Basin. They burned a number of buildings and brush corrals; they tore down fences and let stock intermingle. A great deal of riding was necessary to put cattle back on their proper ranges. Horses were scattered over a wide area, some as far as the Blue Mountains—and horses were needed to separate the cattle. All this happened in the busy summertime when there was plenty of work to do anyway. Ranchers did not get their affairs organized again that year, even those whose headquarters had not been burned.

The Indians did not molest the P Ranch. There the white house, the long barn, and the brush corrals were all left intact.

French's defense of his men at the Diamond Ranch and his leadership of the civilian volunteers in the battle at Silver Creek made some of the best riders in the country proud to work for him. They took up their own homesteads, married, and became well known in their own right. The French-Glenn Company journal lists names still recognized in Harney County, such as, George Bollenbaugh, J. W. Fitzgerald, Gus Harrison, George Hochneadle, William Dillman, William Hudspeth, John G. South, J. Buckmaster, Boland Fine, and Mart Brenton. As young men they helped make French-Glenn efficient and profitable, well manned and well managed.

In the P Ranch account books, the first item noted is the receipt of $400 from Dr. Glenn, probably the sum French had when he started for Oregon. Other payments totaling $976.46 were made by

November of that year. By January 3, 1876, the balance on the books was $15,855.81, although the method of obtaining that balance is obscure. It is not uncommon to find a date on the books out of chronological order, as if there were some afterthought; but that is common with men who keep books only out of necessity and whose minds are busy with the occupation that requires the books. The French accounts do not give a complete record of the little settlement that was the P Ranch, but they seemed to satisfy Dr. Glenn, who demanded no additional records or reports. He knew that his partner's strength did not lie in book work.

Peter French's education was meager, for no schooling beyond the three Rs was then available except in private schools. However, he could read and figure with accuracy, and his handwriting was good, showing practice with a pen. His spelling, though, was by sound rather than rule. Most important, he was remarkably intelligent and had a strong will, so he could learn from experience.

Some of the more involved P Ranch deals did not get into the books at all. On September 13, 1877, French bought the Diamond Swamp from A. H. Robie from whom he had already bought the mill near Fort Harney. The price given is $42,300, or one dollar an acre. The purchase added a big body of deeded land to the French-Glenn holdings. Getting it, though, was a complicated matter; at the time of the sale, it didn't really belong to Robie. He had applied for it under the Swamp Act prior to 1878, when the legislature passed a law restricting sales under the Swamp Act to 320 acres per buyer. Considerable time passed before the regulation was adopted permitting applicants with earlier filings to complete their purchases. The state did not accept final payment from French-Glenn for the swamp until July 20, 1885.

The Diamond Swamp is the biggest swamp in the Harney Basin. It lies north and east of the P Ranch and is a geological extension of the Kiger Gorge, which comes down from the Steens. This deep gorge holds snow water until late summer, providing water for the swamp. In spite of efforts to drain it by French and others, the gorge still remains a partial swamp.

Purchase of the Diamond Swamp brought French into contact and conflict with Darius H. (Rye) Smyth, who would have liked to have had it himself. Smyth was also a settler of 1872, and had lived in Diamond Valley most of that time. Because he refused to sell his holdings, or be moved by French, a sort of feud gradually grew up between the men, the intensity of which has probably been exaggerated by time and the many romanticists who have written about the Steens country.

Rye Smyth was a character of distinction, positive in his views. He did not want to move, nor did he intend to. He refused all offers of money or trade. That he threatened French, or shot the buttons off French's vest, or was threatened by French or someone hired by French, seems better fiction than history. It is not likely that anyone with a knowledge of human nature—of which French possessed a normal amount — would have tried to force big Rye Smyth to do anything. Yet, the two were not always embattled. On several occasions, French asked to adopt Smyth's son Corey (born 1883) and raise him to be his heir. Smyth never permitted it.

French's operation was growing rapidly. He continued to buy cattle and land, and thousands of calves were born each year on the bunchgrass slopes of the Steens. In 1878, he invested $7,560 in cattle and noted a cattle sale of $125,665. In 1879, he invested $10,704 in cattle and sold $23,500 worth. The figures are uneven, but they were probably caused by a fluctuating market. French had around 20,000 head of cattle.

Profit from the cattle business was good in those years, almost fabulously so. Joseph Nimmo, chief of the U. S. Bureau of Statistics, published a bulletin in the early eighties showing that the profit of western stockmen was around twenty per cent. He estimated that there were 800,000 head of cattle in Oregon.

In addition to cattle, Peter French had hundreds of horses and mules, for which there was a steady demand by homesteaders who were coming into the West. Dealers drove bands of horses several hundred miles to settlements, to satisfy the market for work stock.

A horse that had been handled by a white man was a much safer investment for a homesteader than an Indian cayuse, fresh out of the sage, white-eyed and fuzzy-tailed.

On January 28, 1879, Peter French wrote a letter to Dr. Glenn, in which he expressed himself clearly about affairs on the ranch:

DR. GLENN

DEAR SIR,

I wrote you yesterday that I would give you particulars of the sale. The band consisted of 346 steers and 149 cows and heifers and the steers were two and three years old and such cattle as I could not hold. The cows were very good except some pretty old ones. All Diamond Ranch and P cows. Got an average of thirty one dollars and 75/100 per head ($31.75). Think I did well considering that they were range cattle.

Will have use for all the money that they bring and more too. I have obligations to meet by 1st of March to the amount of thirty thousand dollars. Those Kiger debts are due on that date but if I make another sale of cattle I will be able to meet them.

You spoke of taking up that Singletary note. If you do so please write me at Winnemucca.

There are a great many beef cattle in this country still for sale and am afraid that there is not going to be any very great scarcity of beef this season. I would take 8 cents for ours anyway. Have some 2,400 head left.

I wish you would send me from Sacramento five pairs of those chain harness such as you use there on your ranch, two pairs of wheel harness and three pairs of swing. Five pair altogether. Please order them so they will reach here by 10th of Feb. so that my teams will not be delayed. Write to me anyway, would like to know what you got for those cattle you sold, also what cattle there are to go to market yet over there. Regards to family.

(Signed) PETER FRENCH

Among the Glenn papers for the following year, 1880, is a note indicating that there had been a sort of casting up of accounts between French and Glenn and that there were plans for a division of partnership:

French is to receive $55,000 for his interest in the P and Diamond ranches and the cattle on same, provided the cattle count out 8,000 head. If they fall short or overrun that number, $12.00 per head is to be added or deducted from the $55,000 for 1/3 of the number that the cattle overrun, or fall short, the 8,000 head.

French turned over (to Glenn) October 1, 1879, 5,061 head of cattle. His interest amounted to $43,244.00 less his 1/3 share of the indebtedness which was $5,537.38. Therefore, the value of his interest on October 1, 1879 was $37,706.62. Paid French (March 1, 1880) as follows.

Note $28,832.00
Cash   10,000.00
            $38,832.00

This payment also included $1,125.38 in interest, covering the period from October 1, 1879 to March 1, 1880, when Glenn made the settlement. The division of partnership did not take place, but evidently the usual one-third share arrangement was in effect as far as it concerned cattle. French had sold cattle early in 1879 for $31.75 a head, making $12 seem low that fall.

The partners were entering one of the most profitable periods in the history of the French-Glenn Company. French was making large sums of money and Glenn was spending it. Each was good at his job. French himself spent almost nothing. His notations on expenses to Winnemucca and Canyon City show that his personal wants were few. He did buy a home for his parents in Red Bluff, California, and one for his aunts in San Jose, and occasionally he sent money to his sister Mary. With these exceptions, Peter French's money went for land and cattle.

JOHN DEVINE OF WHITE HORSE ∾∾∾∾∾∾∾∾

JOHN DEVINE WAS THE FIRST OF THE CALIFORNIA cattlemen to settle in the Steens Mountain country in Oregon. He was living in the Sacramento Valley, in 1868, when he made arrangements with W. B. Todhunter, a Sacramento butcher, to go to Oregon and explore the possibilities of raising cattle there.

Devine was able to acquire the site of Camp C. F. Smith, which was abandoned in 1869, after three years of occupancy. This site was on a comparatively small oasis, where four creeks flowed through a valley. It was well east of the Pueblo Mountains, south of the Steens. Its terrain was more like Nevada than the Harney Basin. This might have been a deciding factor, because John Devine was familiar with the excellent Nevada cattle on the San Francisco market.

He set up his headquarters by building some permanent houses of native stone, of which there was plenty around. He also constructed a sod house, that is still used, and then put up the famous red barn with the cupola at one end. Atop this he placed the replica of a white horse, thereby giving the name to the ranch and to the largest of the four creeks. The barn and the white horse still exist and are still in good repair.

White Horse Ranch was never a competitor to the P Ranch or the Island Ranch in matters of water, grass, or potential resources. It must depend on small creeks for water, not having the bountiful supply from a snow-fed river.

John S. Devine was a southerner, having been born in Richmond, Virginia, in 1839, just ten years before the birth of Peter

French. Though tall and graceful as a young man, Devine became heavy in later years. All his life he liked race horses. His stallion "Reno" was locally famous and had many colts that were raced in Burns and in California—usually, however, without profit. The big barn on the ranch was really a race-horse barn.

Maurice Fitzgerald, who lived in the region many years and wrote about its history, recorded the following story about Devine. The year was 1874, and a tramp had applied at White Horse Ranch for employment:

> As was his custom, Devine put the man to work doing some chores about the premises. After working for a month, the man asked for his pay and got it, saying he was going south. While he was on the job, a stray horse had wandered in from some distant point. The animal had a brand that no one recognized. As usual in such circumstances, the stray was put into the enclosure with other horses until such time as his owner might happen along and claim him. If no one claimed him, he became the property of the ranch. That was the custom.
>
> The tramp knew of this strange horse, so when he was preparing to leave, he caught the animal and rode off in the direction of Trout Creek.
>
> When Devine learned what the fellow had done, he swore he would never get away with it. Mounting his horse, he started out on the trail of the horse thief. He caught up with him at the ranch of John Catlow on Trout Creek, thirty miles from White Horse. He commanded the tramp to mount his stolen animal and come back with him to the White Horse Ranch.
>
> The horse thief reluctantly obeyed. However, when about half way back, he stopped and said he would go no farther. (He might have feared lynching when he arrived.) Getting off his horse he picked up some large stones and told Devine to return to the home ranch alone, or he would knock him off

his horse. Devine ordered the man to put down the rocks or be shot. The thief called Devine a hard name. Devine fired, and the man dropped in his tracks.

Nothing was done about the killing for two years, according to Fitzgerald. At the end of that time, the authorities in Canyon City notified Devine to come to the county seat—a long four-day trip. At Canyon City, the sheriff was satisfied with Devine's explanation and no action was taken.

Devine and Todhunter were among the first of the big cattlemen to become interested in swamp land. This resulted in their invasion of the Harney Basin and getting control of the Island Ranch east of Burns, but it also resulted in constant conflict with settlers coming into the country. Devine's personality aggravated matters; he had gracious manners for his peers, but none for those of less fortunate circumstances.

He was largely responsible for the many sections of land marked with the big red "S" in the flat area north of Malheur Lake, which was called the "Red S" field. The "S" meant swamp; the lettering was red.

Besides the swamp land wranglings, Devine and Todhunter had other problems. Owners of the Central Oregon Land Grant disputed possession of alternate sections of land because of a Federal land grant for proposed construction of a military road from Albany to Fort Boise. Finally, in 1887, they turned over their property, by trust deed, to Singletary, Hayes, and Brooks of California. Settlers were then clamoring for possession before Oregon officials.

The winter of 1888-1889 struck the final blow. For years prior to this the weather had been very dry. When the hard winter came, there was no hay for the cattle. At least three-fourths of them were lost.

There was no choice but to sell out. Henry Miller bought the remaining cattle and land claims from the creditors. Devine was made superintendent with headquarters on the Island Ranch, but he was not cut out to be second in command. He was a boss. He continued writing Bullhead drafts on Miller until that careful German came up to the ranch and fired him saying, "I never knew a man who could make so many enemies.'

Henry Miller was not vindictive. He let Devine move to the 6,000-acre Alvord Ranch, east of the highest part of the Steens. This was a beautiful ranch, bathed in the myriad, shifting colors of the desert on one side, and shadowed by the rocky heights of Steens Mountain on another. There Devine lived until fatally injured in an accident in 1901.

John Devine made his mark as a big operator of cattle ranches more because of his financial backing than his efficiency or ability to raise quality beef. He liked to have animals about him. His barnyard was always full of horses, chickens, and other domestic animals. At the time of his death he was preserving a small herd of elk on the slopes of the Steens.

THE GLENNS OF JACINTO ~~~~~~~~~~~~~~

MEANWHILE, DR. HUGH J. GLENN WAS BUILDING HIS own empire in California. His farming venture expanded until in 1879, he became known as the world's Wheat King. The *Grizzly Bear*, a reputable California publication, stated that he tilled 65,000 acres of land for wheat and used 1,000 mules and several hundred men in his wheat operations. "He shipped his wheat crop by steamboat from Colusa to Port Costa, Contra Costa County; there it was loaded aboard vessels bound for Liverpool, England, and sold at that port. He did without the services of middlemen, and was considered the wheat baron of the West."

Certainly no one in the nineteenth century could compete with Dr. Glenn in the production of wheat. His well-advertised operations made huge borrowings necessary, his reputation made them possible, and his credit was good. Occasionally he exerted ruthless pressure on small farmers to get them to sell. Merchants were eager to know him because he was constantly buying machinery or having it built. He was in the market for ships and barges to move the million bushels of wheat he was said to grow; and for warehouses in which to store it.

In politics, Dr. Glenn was a Democrat, but he took little part in such affairs until, in 1879, he was nominated for governor of the New Constitution Party, a dissident offshoot of the national organization. That same year, he was also nominated for the office by the Democrats, to become the only New Constitution man to be so recognized. Some observers believed this was the result of his wealth and his willingness to spend it, to obtain not only his own election but that of others on the ticket. Glenn's own loyalties were divided between the two branches of the party.

The election was unusually bitter, many regular Democrats being violently opposed to Glenn's affiliation with the New Constitution group. He received almost no newspaper support. The year of 1879 proved to be a bad one for Democrats in California. When George C. Gorman, a prominent Republican, came out for Glenn, even more Democrats were alienated, but the worst came when a workingman's party was organized. It attacked Glenn, charging that he owned 65,000 acres of land and hired Chinamen to farm it. Anti-Chinese sentiment was high and hiring Chinese labor was far from a political asset.

The Sacramento *Daily Record,* on August 2, 1879, published an editorial about Glenn that could have brought no comfort to his supporters. It is a sort of model of vituperative political writing. It read in part:

> During his brief and not glorious political career he has already demonstrated a talent for shuffling and equivocating which would not have discredited a much older politician . . . All who know him are convinced he prefers the cheapest labor he can get, and that he would rather have slave labor than any other. . . .

As if to clinch the argument once and for all, another editorial, in the same issue and on the same page, read:

> He lends money at 18% that he borrowed at 9%, pays about 9 cents an hour for labor which starts at half past three in the morning and goes on until nine at night, is not paid promptly, is paid by check, and discounted . . . (He) excludes civilization from his domain.

The paper further noted that Glenn was in debt $1,200,000. The doctor undoubtedly had supporters of his candidacy, but unfortunately not many of them were writing for the newspapers. The party was split, with another candidate named White, who called himself a Democrat. However—likely because his name was so well known—Glenn did not fare too badly in the election. The winner was George C. Perkins, Republican, with 67,970 votes; Glenn received 47,562, and White 44,620. Everything considered, it was a fair showing for a newcomer in politics running as a candidate of a divided party. He managed to carry Colusa County; and his neighbors supported him—in his own Jacinto there were but three votes against him. Apparently those with a closer knowledge of the doctor's practices held different views from the *Daily Record.*

Glenn's defeat was inevitable, but the doctor was not the type to let politics discourage him in his business affairs. He was a good example of the nineteenth century plunger and promoter who could direct his energy with practical shrewdness—and his energy was boundless. He crossed the country with stock on a dozen trips, when one such trip was enough for most men. He bought the Jacinto tract and increased it; and he bought horses and mules by the hundreds. Everything he did was in the grand manner. He built the largest home, ran for the highest state office, drank immoderately and occasionally gambled for high stakes. And, he did it all on borrowed money.

Though the doctor had a fine house at Jacinto, he bought a mansion for his family in Oakland at the corner of Jackson and Lake streets, paying $65,000 for property that had reportedly cost $125,000 a few years before. The family move to Oakland probably delighted his daughter, Ella, who, in that crossroads years of 1879, was a senior at Mills Seminary in that same city.

One likely reason for the move was that the doctor had become involved with a Mrs. C. B. Posten. He gave her a job discounting the checks of the men, who, as the Sacramento *Daily Record* had noted, were paid by check. As there was no bank nearby, the only way to cash them was through her, and she required a fee for the service.

On one of Peter French's trips to California with a load of cattle, he paid his usual visit to the Glenns. The grandeur of their new home awed the Oregon cowman and the flirtatious charm of their pretty daughter Ella captured his heart.

In her imposing home at Jackson and Lake, Ella was married to Peter French, February 1, 1883. At the ceremony, he used John William, the name his parents gave him, rather than the name Peter, which he had called himself for twelve years.

Peter French was now a man of thirty-three, small, wiry, experienced with cows if not with women, dapper, unschooled, an outdoors man, and fitted only for life there. Ella was a small, well-rounded, red-haired woman of twenty-two, a lover of luxury, entirely unfitted for hardship. Peter was interested in cattle and making money; she in spending it. It is doubtful if this young woman had more than passing interest in the finest traits of this swarthy cowman from the Steens.

The gala wedding was duly noted in the San Francisco *Call*, and the Oakland *Tribune* followed with an account a few days later, describing the bride as a graduate of Mills Seminary, and the only daughter of Dr. Hugh James Glenn, the great farmer of Colusa County, and the Democratic nominee for governor of the state in 1879. The account gave details of the beautiful parlors, richly decorated with the choicest flowers, where at half past eight, the Reverend T. H. B. Anderson read the ceremony. The bride herself was "attired in a crushed strawberry dress of corded silk and brocaded satin, adorned with point lace and tasteful flowers." The contrast between the pair must have been great. Only a short time before, the groom had been branding calves in a dusty corral in a still unsettled part of Oregon.

Guests at the wedding were nearly all Glenns, but, oddly enough, also present was John G. South, sometime bookkeeper and cowhand at the P Ranch and later a business man in the bay area. Peter's sister Mary was also there, but she was the only member of the groom's family in attendance.

One paper said the newlyweds were to leave on an eastern bridal tour, but they didn't. After visiting members of both families at Jacinto and Red Bluff, the newlyweds started for the Oregon country, planning to visit San Francisco and Winnemucca en route.

But, even before the echoes of the wedding bells died, there were predictions that the marriage would not be a success.

DEATH CAME SUDDENLY TO DR. HUGH JAMES GLENN. On Saturday, February 17, 1883, between two and three o'clock in the afternoon, he was walking on the porch of his Jacinto Hotel, watching his men catch a horse that had broken loose with harness on. Without warning, he was shot in the head by Huram Miller, his recently discharged bookkeeper. The charge from Miller's double-barreled shotgun tore away a part of the doctor's parietal bone, above and a little behind his right ear, together with a part of the brain as large as an egg. It was a mortal wound.

Till the time of his death at 8:57 that same evening, Glenn spoke only twice; he asked why the doctor hadn't come. Members of the family near enough to be summoned were at his bedside.

The Oakland *Tribune* reported that after the shooting, Miller ran from the porch toward the brick store, then west across a field, waving his gun. R. M. Cochran, a ranch foreman, and John Morran pursued him in a buggy. When the men came near the fleeing Miller and shouted for him to surrender, he pointed his gun at Cochran.

Cochran was armed with a Henry rifle. Passing the lines to Morran, he shot into the ground near Miller and again asked him to surrender. Miller refused and Cochran shot him in the leg above the knee, but Miller still would not surrender. He kept his gun until Cochran threatened again, whereupon he cast his shotgun aside and was captured. He was taken to Willows for his wound to be dressed.

The justice of the peace placed Miller under arrest, charged with murder, and ordered him removed to Colusa, the county seat. There Miller refused to talk other than to say that Cochran had done right in shooting him. The transfer to Colusa was necessary precaution against a lynching.

Miller and Glenn had been boys together, the *Tribune* reported, and Mrs. Miller and Mrs. Glenn had been warm friends since girlhood. Dr. Glenn had often helped provide for the Miller family when Miller was on one of his drinking sprees. He had even set him up in business in Jacinto, because Miller was very capable when sober. However, Miller soon fell to drinking again and Glenn had to let him go.

Miller had run through several other jobs before Glenn hired him as bookkeeper. His other bookkeeper had quit because of the check-shaving activities of Mrs. Posten. The doctor apparently thought that Miller would accept Mrs. Posten's practice. He didn't and was fired. That same day, Miller obtained a shotgun in Willows, saying that he would raffle it off to make some money.

The shooting of Dr. Glenn roused newspapers throughout Northern California to high praise of the man. The *Tribune* wrote:

> Dr. Hugh J. Glenn, of Colusa, was one of the remarkable men of his age. He was born to be a leader in whatever he undertook. Had he commenced his business career in Wall Street, he could have been another Commodore Vanderbilt or Jay Gould. Had he started life as a merchant he would have been another A. T. Stewart. Educated as a physician, an unexpected event made him a land holder, and in a few years he became the largest farmer on the globe, and the only wheat grower in America who chartered his own ships and sold by telegraph his own grain to Europe, dispensing with middlemen entirely. His payments for labor and supplies on his ranch have reached as high as $600,000 in a single year.

He was acclaimed a near-perfect physical specimen, without a weak spot in his well-knit body. It was said that he could ride a mule eighteen hours a day when supervising his vast holdings. In addition to his thousands of acres in California, Glenn was credited with ownership of 70,000 acres of land in Oregon, stocked with 30,000 cattle which he had never seen.

Peter and Ella were at Winnemucca, on their way to Oregon, when notified of her father's death. They returned immediately to Oakland for the funeral.

The funeral of the murdered doctor, on Tuesday, February 20, was an elaborate affair held in the carved walnut rooms of his ornate Oakland home. His body was laid to rest in Mountain View Cemetery on the hills above Oakland, but was later transferred to a private cemetery in Jacinto.

Glenn's estate, including real and personal property, amounted to $1,232,678, a very sizable estate to be left by anyone, and a mark of success on the part of the doctor. The bond of S. E. Wilson, the administrator, was set at $250,000. Stories circulated that the debts of the estate would exceed the assets, but none of the stories of impending financial ruin impressed the family, which drew on the administrator for money every month.

There is no list of Glenn's creditors at the time of his death, though there is a record that Glenn obtained a credit of a million dollars from Lazard Freres of San Francisco; also that E. C. Singletary, a money lender to large borrowers, loaned Glenn huge sums, once receiving $70,703 in principal and interest in one payment. But Glenn's principal asset was himself. Without his personal management there was no certainty that the business would continue or even that the debts would be paid.

After the funeral, Peter French returned to Oregon alone. Ella had decided to stay in California, to be with her mother. The family was grief stricken and bewildered—but still determined to go on spending money as recklessly as before.

Ella was more like her father than any of the boys and had taken more interest in him and his work. She not only had an education superior to the average, but she also had ambition and the shrewdness to further it. Her marriage to Peter seems to have been one of convenience; she treated it as such. With the death of her father, it also became financial security.

But evidence that she never came to Oregon, and never lived with Peter French on the Oregon ranch, is more convincing than that she did.

THE LAW AND HURAM MILLER

THE TRIAL OF HURAM MILLER FOR THE FIRST-degree murder of Dr. Hugh Glenn was held late in June, 1883, in Colusa, with Jackson Hatch, one-time employer of Miller, as attorney for his defense. Hatch was adept at using the evidence and improvising innuendo to impress the jury. Mr. Hatch saw to it that Mrs. Posten, also known as Mrs. C. B. Dyer, had a prominent place in the trial. Dr. Glenn had been disappointed in Miller's assumption of a moral attitude regarding the check shaving, without considering that it was Miller who had to face the anger of the men. Miller did protest and was actually fired on the complaint of Mrs. Posten that Miller had not discounted enough. J. C. Jones, who succeeded Miller, testified that $2,007 had been transferred to Mrs. Posten to aid her in the discounting of checks.

The prosecution argued that Miller had not denied that he shot and killed Glenn and that he was guilty of murder. Jackson Hatch, in his turn, recited threats Glenn had made on the life of Miller because of differences with Mrs. Posten.

The jury disagreed, standing eight to four for murder in the second degree. After three days, the judge finally discharged them. Jackson Hatch had done his job well. A second trial was held in October, but without Jackson Hatch; and on the 25th, Huram Miller was found guilty of murder in the first degree, with punishment fixed at imprisonment for life. He entered Folsom prison on October 30, 1883, and remained there until December 9, 1890, when his sentence was commuted to fifteen years by Governor Robert W. Waterman "because of the evidence of the trial." On January 3, 1891, Miller was discharged.

But Huram Miller had put an end to the glory of the Glenns, a glory that had lasted sixteen years. Shortly after the first trial of

107

Miller, Carrie B. Posten filed a claim against the Glenn estate for $6,437.65 to shock the administrator, S. E. Wilson, and the court. However, the following week she withdrew the claim and stepped out of the picture forever. She, too, played an important part in hastening the disintegration of the Glenn family.

The death of Dr. Glenn made a difference in the management of the P Ranch as well as in the conduct of affairs at Jacinto. Creditors did not think Wilson was the right man for the job of settling the huge estate, which consisted of ranches in three states, thousands of cattle, as well as an expensive family to support and much indebtedness. N. D. Rideout, of the Butte County bank, itself one of the major creditors, replaced Wilson, April 2, 1885, managing the property until his death. F. C. Lusk, an attorney of Chico, who often represented the bank, then took over and served until all debts were paid. Lusk was a small, brusque, single man, who made something of a record at handling the affairs of large companies.

A record of cattle sold shows that French marketed more stock than usual during the first years after Glenn's death, in an apparent effort to pay off some of the more pressing debts and reduce the interest charges.

If French were to have received a third of the increase, he would soon have been getting a third of the proceeds of sales, at least in four years. This was not the case; he never did get a third. One might wonder why French stayed on under such circumstances. He was the competent member of the partnership where cow management was concerned; he knew cows and he knew the range in the Blitzen Valley. He could have borrowed the money to buy the spread, if Glenn had been willing to sell—which he wasn't. Then, after Glenn's death, the creditors would not sell the most profitable and only solvent part of the assets.

The reason Peter French stayed on cannot be found in financial considerations, only in spiritual. These reasons were loyalty and ambition. In Oregon on the P Ranch, French was akin to royalty. He had power and position—and the history of man is that he will suffer almost anything for these.

PETER FRENCH THE MAN

IN THE YEAR OF GLENN'S DEATH, PETER FRENCH had been in Oregon eleven years, and had become boss of one of the largest and best-managed cattle spreads in the West. He was respected by his contemporaries. Rancher Henry Miller envied him his location, calling it the best in the country. John Devine wished he had French's drive and ambition.

Most of the things that have been written about French are by those who never saw him, were prejudiced for or against him, or who had little understanding of the country or the times. Efforts to romanticize—or disparage—him have been numerous.

Among those who knew him personally, pioneer stockman Bill Hanley—who came first to Grant County in 1879—had this to say:

> French was the outstanding one of them all. A little dapper man with his cane, he looked like a dancing master. Slim built and wiry, he never weighed over 125 pounds, and had very dark hair and skin and very brilliant eyes. He was all business, active and quick in decisions, always the real boss, and he knew the country and everything in it. A splendid vaquero, he was good with the rope and preferred a well-worn saddle.
>
> He brought up many of the best vaqueros of California, and every one of his men had his own string of good saddle horses and the best vaquero equipment. They were all under control, but always loyal to the boss. A hard worker, he kept himself going, and everyone else too.

109

Archie McGowan—son of storekeeper George McGowan, who named Burns—used to say that Peter French was responsible for the development of Harney County, for without his drive and foresight it could never have become the successful cattle country it is.

McGowan described Peter French this way:

He was a bundle of nerves and was both loved and hated. Most men who worked for him admired and respected him, but he was a driver. He was not so much a man to talk as he was to act. He built fences as fine and straight as an arrow sixty years ago, and some of them are standing today. His willow corrals were models.

Peter also took pride in his appearance, always kept neat and clean. He was not a drinking man and did not approve of gambling.

Although the reputation of Peter French has been shaped to fit the fiction writer's conception of a land-hungry overlord, evidence to justify that characterization is insufficient. As long as control was in his hands he had little trouble with the stockmen or settlers who lived in the Blitzen Valley or around Malheur Lake, although there were some disputes. French engaged in local affairs and experienced the usual disagreements, but no more than could be expected.

French liked to dance and women liked to dance with him—whether because of his grace, or his reputation for success. Dances were a popular form of entertainment in the late nineteenth century, with most of them held in homesteaders' or settlers' cabins. The scanty furniture was stacked outside and the fiddler was perched in a corner above the dancers. When Burns grew large enough to support a dance hall, French attended dances there.

There are stories that French was a ladies' man. Dave Shirk recalled a sort of contest between himself and French for the favors of a lady of the community, the result of which caused Shirk to hold eternal enmity toward the victor. All this seems reasonable and natural. Liking women detracts from no man. There are a few old wives' tales that his interest in the fair sex occasionally exceeded propriety, but, truth or fiction, it would not have been out of character, nor in conflict with the customs of his day.

He was well acquainted in Burns, patronized its stores, hobnobbed with its citizens, and attended parties of young folk. Though must older, he was always a welcome addition. Wherever something was going on, he could usually be found, for he was impatient at inactivity. When Peter came to town, small boys flocked around because he passed out silver dollars to them in the manner of some grandee—and such was his background that he could have seen himself in that role.

French was always a regular contributor to the Methodist Church in Burns, especially to the Christmas program when gifts were distributed to children. And, he was quick to help those in trouble. Once, when he was in Burns, a house caught on fire.

Townsmen rushed to the scene with buckets. While some pumped water from the well, others carried it. French climbed atop the house, better to direct the distribution of water. Missing his step, he fell to the ground. Typically, he shook himself and climbed back onto the roof.

Grover Jameson recalls that when French drove in from the P Ranch—often in one day with a change of horses at the Sod House Ranch—he would ask the boys to wait a few minutes. Then he would cross the street from the livery stable to the Trish & Donegan saloon to get a pocketful of silver dollars, one for each boy.

The family of George McGowan went often to the white house in the French buckboard. Then the "boss" would help Mrs. McGowan and the children into his rig and drive them home because he liked the children. He gave trinkets to little boys who came to his house, if they were very small; and he took them riding with him if they were large enough to handle a pony. He talked along with them about interesting things and let them do small errands to stimulate their desire for responsibility. Peter French was a gentleman, and with small boys he was a gentle man; but that did not prevent his pursuing his own way in business, to the occasional discomfort of other men. A man may be easy with colts and stern with older horses that are supposed to know what to do.

And Peter French liked music. Julian Byrd—former editor of the Burns *Times-Herald* and son of the first editor—used to tell of his visits to the P Ranch as a boy, and of riding over the country in a buckboard with the "big boss." Together they would sing ballads they knew of the cattle trails. Cowboy songs, as they are now known, were not yet written and probably would not have been sung by a cowman of 1880. But French, then in his thirties and Julian Byrd, still in his teens, may have harmonized over "Buffalo Gal" and "Sweet Betsy From Pike."

French gave young Julian the run of the P Ranch, and years later Julian recalled one of French's little jokes:

> He told me to hunt anything on his ranch but never shoot a quail. One day I killed a crane. Pete said it was a mighty fine bird and that we would have to eat it. All through dinner Pete spoke of what a nice crane it was. I didn't want to eat it, but found that what was on my plate tasted wonderful. It wasn't until afterwards I found out that it was one of Pete's pranks. He had the Chinese cook get rid of the crane and serve turkey instead.

An old cow hand of Harney County recalled that, when he was a boy in his teens, he rode south from the Grande Ronde Valley to see a bit of the world and eventually reached the Blitzen Valley with a tired horse and an empty stomach. Riding across a flat, he was suddenly surrounded by a bunch of wolf hounds, and Peter French rode up on a big horse to inquire what he was doing there. When the cow hand explained his presence, French told him to drop in at any of his camps for a meal. The man later worked on the P Ranch for many years.

The keeping of wolf hounds to hunt coyotes was common in Eastern Oregon, among men who liked the sport of watching the dogs catch and disintegrate a coyote, after a long chase that men could follow on horseback—if well mounted. Coyotes were the arch enemy of French's cattle.

The house French built on the P Ranch apparently just grew. He did not have title to the land until 1882, and by that time was in need of a larger house than the small quarters in which he lived during his first years in Oregon. The single-story part of the house in the center was but sixteen feet wide. The second-story section to the right (west) was presumably French's bedroom. The eastern two-story part of the house was a later addition, built after there was more need to entertain business and personal guests, nearly all of whom stayed overnight because there were no other accommodations within seventy miles.

It was essentially a bachelor's house, owned and occupied by a solitary man, and kept by a Chinese cook. Nevertheless, Peter French had some fine things in his home. There were some beautiful pieces of furniture and some excellent leather goods, along with some grotesque bits. "Bruss" Byrd remembered an old chair, in the white house on the P Ranch, in which he was permitted to sit when, as a boy, he visited there. It was made of cow horns, with feet of hooves and arms of huge horns.

In these comfortable headquarters, French kept his books on engineering, his tracts on cattle and their management, and his pamphlets on irrigation and drainage. He was a cattleman who never guessed about management and improvement, he studied it. Visiting cattlemen and cattle buyers were glad to be invited to visit in the home of the boss of the Blitzen.

With all his conviviality, French was a lonely man, as bosses usually are. Yet he had plenty of business problems to occupy his thoughts, as well as the management of thousands of acres of land and thousands of head of cattle and horses. His work required daily—almost hourly—attention. To handle all this, while at the same time paying off the Glenn notes, was a burden French made no effort to evade. Glenn had given him his start; he would help the family. Marriage to Ella strengthened a loyalty already present. Friends advised him to branch out for himself — which he undoubtedly could have done—but he refused.

HENRY MILLER THE BUTCHER

TO A COWMAN, A COW IS A SORT OF FELLOW creature that must be carefully tended, provided with proper food and water, cared for in sickness, and kept from emotional disturbances that can make her dangerous. When she is sold, the cowman follows her up the ramp to the freight car with a touch of guilt in his heart; for mere pelf he is parting with something he liked and respected.

To a butcher, a cow is so many sirloin steaks, so much boiling beef, a few dollars' worth of hide, and a few cents worth of hair. Butchers can estimate the gross value of a cow at a glance. She is an article of commerce, like a sack of cement or a bushel of wheat.

By such standards, Peter French was the cowman; Henry Miller the butcher. Miller made more money out of cows than any of the stockmen of his time. He came to own stock ranches and herds of cattle, but basically he remained a butcher.

Miller was a German trained from childhood to be an efficient worker, a hater of waste or laziness.

Born July 21, 1827, in Wurttemberg, Germany, to parents whose name was Kreiser, he began herding calves for his father as soon as he could walk fast enough. From his father he learned the butcher's trade. After the death of his parents, the lad made his way to New York. There he worked in a butcher shop until, by chance, he bought a ticket for California, from a young man named Henry Miller, who had abandoned his desire to join the gold rush. Because the ticket was made out to Henry Miller and stamped "Not

Transferable," young Kreiser assumed the name on the ticket for the trip—and so fancied it that he used it the rest of his life.

In San Francisco, he quickly found a job and soon even had a shop of his own. Within a few years he was making trips into the San Joaquin Valley to buy cattle. In 1858, he formed a partnership with Charles Lux, an Alsatian, also in the butcher business, but Lux was a different sort of man. He catered to and associated with the nabobs who lived on San Francisco's seven hills, and ran the banks and businesses of the city. Lux could always get money, and when the firm began to buy land in the San Joaquin valley, Miller needed huge sums of it. The Miller & Lux firm prospered, for it had the income from growing cattle, as well as from butchering and retailing the meat.

Miller started irrigation systems, built dams, and continued to purchase land—until the company owned the better part of the valley. He hired lawyers by the score to fight his continual battles in the courts, importuned legislators, bulled his hard way through many difficult situations—and he won most of the time by hook or crook. Lux stood by, tolerant and helpful until his death in 1887. A long legal battle with the heirs ensued but Miller finally won. In all matters his methods were ruthless.

When settlers invaded the San Joaquin Valley, the land became more useful for farming than for grazing. Miller then looked for new grazing lands. He went to Nevada, along the Walker River, where N. H. A. "Hock" Mason was trying to start a big cattle spread. Miller loaned him money. When Mason headed north to establish the Quinn River Ranch, he was again aided by Miller, and the 7S brand was put on the tender hides of thousands of calves. Mason went broke — having been too extended in some bad years — and Miller took over the ranches.

Miller also lent money to Tom Overfelt, who had some cattle along the North Fork of the Malheur River in Oregon. Overfelt had met Miller in San Francisco, while on a cattle-selling trip. With Miller's money he continued to buy and grow cattle until he was killed in 1886. Miller then added Overfelt's outfit to his own and moved into the Harney Basin. Overfelt's brand was LF, with the F backwards.

By 1890, Miller had taken over the Todhunter & Devine outfit, when that firm was caught in dry years, topped by a hard winter. Thus the S Wrench brand was added to Miller & Lux ownership. Miller was now able to boast that he could drive cattle from the Blue Mountains of Oregon to San Francisco—and stop on his own land each night.

No one made money dealing with Henry Miller. He was a hard man in a trade. He annoyed his superintendents and foremen with continual carping criticism about minor details of running stock. This stock included more than cattle. Miller also raised hogs, sheep, and poultry to supply his butcher shops in California.

He could estimate the weight of a cow within ten pounds and determine her value accurately. He used Hereford and Devon bulls on the prevailing Shorthorn cows because they rustled better. Miller could not abide laziness in either man or beast.

After he had taken over the Devine holdings in Oregon, he formed the Pacific Livestock Company, which at one time owned the greater part of the Silvies Valley, but settlers frustrated his desire to own the whole valley, finally forcing him to open some ten thousand acres to them and pay $125,000 to the state for encroachment of swamp land—which really wasn't swamp land at all.

Henry Miller wanted everything, but if he couldn't get it now, he would wait and plan to get it later. He held no grudges that interfered with business. Small stockmen could use his bulls—if they sold him the beef. When Henry Miller died in 1916, at the age of 89, he had amassed a fortune, but he died as he had lived—a butcher not a cowman.

SETTLERS OF HARNEY BASIN 〰〰〰〰〰

THE RAILROAD REACHED ONTARIO EARLY IN 1883, but even before that, men were coming into the Harney Basin looking for land. Many of these were farm lads from the Middle Border, used to growing corn and determined to make a start in a new country. Some even had money. The Harney Basin was strange to them, higher and drier, and larger in perspective than anything in Iowa.

They were willing to work and were good help on the ranches, but they wanted land of their own. Furthermore, they knew that the government was glad to give them 160 acres of land under the provisions of the Homestead Act of 1862. That act was hailed as a fine move to provide heads of families with land on which to raise a family, but it didn't work that way. For years the government made no provision for the vastly different kinds of western land. A quarter section in a fertile river bottom was indeed a generous gift; a similar estate on a barren prairie was a trap from which many did not escape. Many of the homesteads were not worth taking. They could not produce enough for a family, even with the heroic skimping done by most homesteaders' wives.

Because United States industry could not absorb all citizens available for work, men stayed with agriculture, even though the price of farm products was low. Taking a homestead seemed a natural prelude to starting a farm, and an idle young man who had not exercised his homestead rights was considered something of a sluggard.

Homesteading was not a remedy for social or economic ills, and no doubt it engendered as much misery as it allayed. But, men in the East continued to hear of the fabulous valley at the foot of the Steens Mountain — where a cowman had built himself a great ranch — and they were curious and envious. They came to do likewise. Besides, after the defeat of the Indians in 1878, the Harney Basin was considered safe for settlers. The tribes had been dispersed to faraway reservations.

Not everyone who took up a homestead did so because he expected to farm it, run stock on it, or even live on it; not every homesteader was a prospective granger. Many a man took up a homestead because he could sell it at a profit. He could live in his bare cabin the minimum number of days—or even less, if he were on such good terms with his homesteading neighbors that they would swear he had stayed the required time. When he made proof, the land was his as evidenced by a lithographed patent from the Federal government. If he chose to sell the land, that was his own business. And sell it he often did. He had fulfilled the rules: he had built a house, put up a fence, slept there as required, and had kept his extra coat there as proof of occupancy.

Peter French purchased many such homesteads, some of them from men who worked for him. The record seems clear that he paid good prices for this land—and that is probably the only way he got it. Almost every large western ranch grew this way, and landowners were not criticized for their tactics. It was not illegal.

Prior to 1880, there were only a few families in the south end of Grant County, other than those working for the big cow outfits. Those who did come into the country to settle wanted the fertile land in the bottoms. On the hills there was seldom enough water to produce crops. They took up land along the Silvies and pushed across the Narrows, or by Windy Point, onto the broad expanse of land immediately south of Malheur Lake. This was neither fenced nor surveyed—nor is it even today. The land was open to anyone, and it was fertile in spots. These settlers were especially welcome to the local merchants. In the eighties there was hardly a western town that did not view the day when it would be a second Denver or Omaha, with stockyards and packing plants and factories filling adjacent prairies. There were difficulties though. The best land was already claimed by stockmen who had been there ten years or more and held title through use and priority. Nevertheless, merchants could figure and, for customers, they preferred a hundred half-starved homesteaders to one big cowman and his outfit.

Remnants of settlers' cabins can still be seen in sagebrush deserts that will not support a half dozen cows on a quarter section. East of the Steens, the rock walls of their store buildings and meeting houses linger as monuments to the home-building ambitions of a misguided generation. In their failure, homesteaders proved that Harney County is best suited to use by big outfits.

The position of the homesteaders, even along the lake, was economically very difficult. The elevation there is 4,100 feet, which means that few crops can be matured. Often the grains must be used for hay and not threshed, and only the hardiest vegetables will grow year after year. The only safe crop is hay for cattle and sheep; but cattlemen would not permit sheep to survive. Furthermore, large ranchers had the range corralled and somehow cattle with strange brands did not seem to do very well.

Peter French was more lenient with the settlers than most of the stockmen, perhaps because he had more. He permitted their cows to run on the lower Blitzen meadows, as long as none of his cattle were taken out with them. As any big rancher knew, homesteaders did not like the taste of their own beef.

French also gave settlers work when it was available. He never tried to dislodge them and stood ready to buy them out at good prices when they wanted to sell land to which they held title. He even marketed their stock for them. As a result, they liked and respected him. Nearly all the evidence, during the eighties, of conflict between French and the settlers was manufactured as part of a later quarrel.

Peter French's sprawling P Ranch, in the Valley of the Donner und Blitzen, is now part of the 184,000-acre Malheur National Wildlife Refuge, one of the country's greatest waterfowl nesting grounds. The refuge includes Malheur, Mud, and Harney lakes, the Double-O, or OO Ranch, as well as the Blitzen Valley. It embraces magnificent scenic vistas with acres of lakes, marshes, meadows, hills and picturesque rimrock country. More than 230 species of birds already have been recorded here.

Visitors will hear the whistling swan, the cooing call of the Wilson's phalarope, the evening flight song of the snipe, and the irate protests of the willets.

Here where French's thousands of head of cattle once fed—to be fattened for Winnemucca's markets—stately avocets stalk about the shallows, and long-billed curlews frequent the salt-grass flats.

Bureau of Sport Fisheries and Wildlife
By David B. Marshall

Springtime mating dance of the Sandhill cranes.

Bureau of Sport Fisheries and Wildlife
By David B. Marshall

Caspian terns along the shore of Harney Lake—sometimes called sea swallows because of their graceful, dashing flight.

Bureau of Sport Fisheries and Wildlife
By Ray C. Erickson

Trumpeter swans near refuge headquarters. These elegant creatures are famous for their ringing, resonant voice.

Bureau of Sport Fisheries and Wildlife
By David B. Marshall

Snowy egret with her young, in a nest in hard-stem bulrush at Malheur Lake. At one time, the species became very rare because of pursuit of the lovely, long white plumes, which grow during breeding season. When the adult birds are killed for these, the young are left to die.

Thousands of pintail, or river ducks, at the peak of fall migration.

Bureau of Sport Fisheries and Wildlife
By David B. Marshall

Forster's tern, at nest here, is easily recognized by the characteristic black cap.

Bureau of Sport Fisheries and Wildlife
By David B. Marshall

Male sage grouse struts proudly before two hens. This grouse's favorite food is the buds of sagebrush—as his name suggests.

Charles Conkling

Young pelicans pant in the sun while their parents fly away to fish in Malheur Lake.

Bureau of Sport Fisheries and Wildlife
By Ray C. Erickson

Nesting colony of cliff swallows in rimrock west of Crow Cabin. This species—often called eaves swallows—builds its bottle-like nest of mud against cliffs or under eaves.

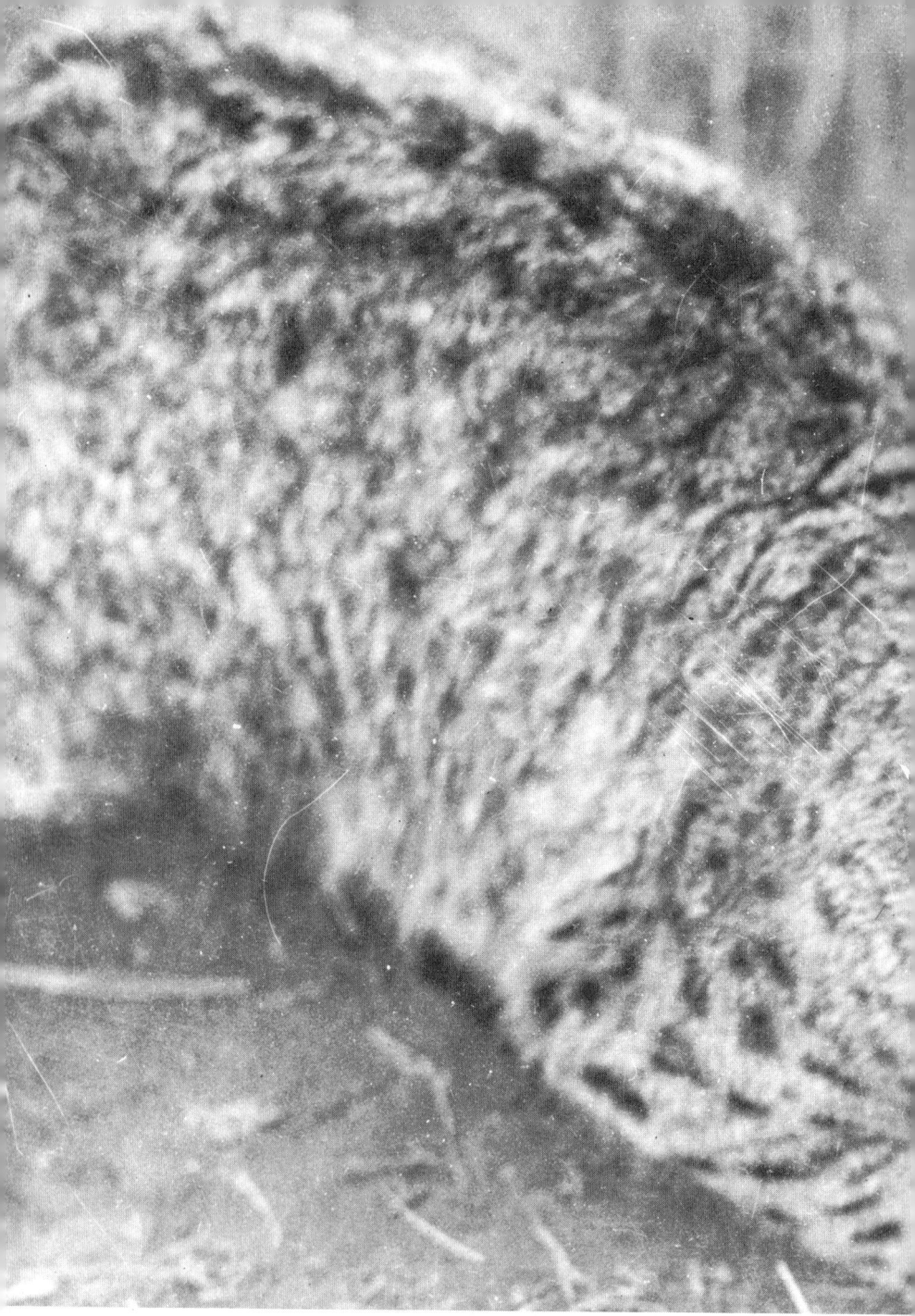

Close-up of a bobcat at Malheur Refuge. When Peter French's vaqueros were riding the ranges to look after cattle, they often packed a rifle because of these predators that killed calves and destroyed game. *Inset:* A bobcat surveys the P Ranch country.

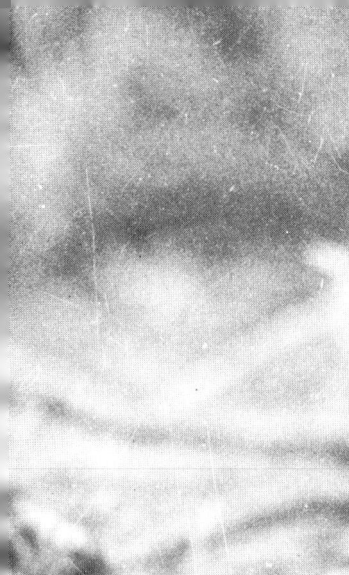

Bureau of Sport Fisheries and Wildlife
By Ray C. Erickson
Inset by David B. Marshall

Bureau of Sport Fisheries and Wildlife
By Ray C. Erickson

Canada goose flushing from nest in cat-tails at Buena Vista Pond. Note the black head and neck, and a continuous white patch from the sides of the head under the throat—characteristics of this common wild goose.

Bureau of Sport Fisheries and Wildlife
By Ray C. Erickson

Canada goose nest and goslings on a small island in Buena Vista Pond.

Bureau of Sport Fisheries and Wildlife
By David B. Marshall

Male antelope with his harem, in a refuge meadow. Tawny above and white below, they also usually show a white rump patch.

The proud pronghorn antelope is found throughout the sagebrush areas of Southeastern Oregon.

Bureau of Sport Fisheries and Wildlife
By Ray C. Erickson

Mule deer at the P Ranch. Note the large ears that give them a mule-like appearance.

The Desert Evening Primrose blooms in clusters on some of the more barren areas of the Peter French country.

Left: The dainty, small-flowered Fringe-Cup is another of the lovely blooms to be found east of the Cascades, where it prefers the moister regions.

Right: One of the most famous western flowers is the Mariposa Lily, or Sego Lily. Its delicate purple blossoms are common among the sagebrush and rocky drylands of the Peter French country.

Bureau of Sport Fisheries and Wildlife
By E. P. Haddon

A cougar peers out at a white world from a snow-covered treetop in the Steens Mountain country.

Bureau of Sport Fisheries and Wildlife
By Ray C. Erickson

Like the cougar above, this member of "Rattlesnake Den"—about four miles south of the Malheur headquarters—is an arch enemy of the native birdlife. He is a rather sluggish fellow, not inclined to bite—except in search of prey.

FRENCH RAN THE RANCHES AS IF THEY WERE HIS own private domain. That is what Dr. Glenn expected and wanted while alive. Sometimes he purchased land in his own name and left it there for years, transferring it to the company when convenient. Records do not show that French obtained income from rental or sale of land, but they do show that occasionally he sold land to French-Glenn at higher prices than he paid for it. Such was Peter French's independence. He was the ranch manager and boss of the cow outfit. The firm owned upwards of 70,000 acres of land, some of it bottom land that needed irrigation or draining, but more of it range land with such varying elevations that it had to be grazed at different times to get the most feed from it. The cattle count ran to 45,000 head, the chief source of income at the P Ranch.

After the purchase of the Diamond Swamp in 1877, French moved on down the Blitzen Valley, buying land whenever it was for sale, and steadily pushing on toward Malheur Lake.

Until 1881, Malheur Lake had no outlet, remaining full in the summer until evaporation lowered it. Martin H. Brenton, who rode for French and other cattlemen, testified that he was on the Sand Reef between Harney and Malheur Lakes one day that year when Malheur Lake reached the top of this barrier. He said he kicked some sand around until the water began to flow westward into Harney Lake, the smaller lake in the Harney Basin. Some persons support Brenton's statement; others say the, action started from natural causes. Still Brenton swore to it. Yet, no matter who or what caused Malheur to start flowing into Harney, the effect was the lowering of Malheur Lake. Lowering by just a foot exposed more than 10,000 acres of land.

Both Silvies and Blitzen are rivers that discharge a large part of their water during the spring runoff. The Silvies Valley may be a marsh in May and as dry as a powder house by July. In summer, when the water from these rivers was used for irrigation—and always after the snow water ran from the Blue Mountains and the Steens—Malheur Lake shrank rapidly. The drainage into Harney Lake and evaporation combined to remove the water.

Irrigation was one of Peter French's innovations. He had men dig ditches to channel the water of the Blitzen River, especially below the Diamond Swamp, out over the parts of the valley floor where sagebrush grew instead of meadow grass. Sage will not live, even for a short time, if its roots are under water, and flooding eradicates it. French improved hundreds of acres with this method; he made the swamp lands drier and the sage flats wetter, to the benefit of both. His irrigation projects of themselves held the water of Malheur Lake at a lower level, causing more dry land between the water and the meander line. The meander line is a surveyed line which follows the outline of some given stream, lake, or swamp. Such lines were later to have profound impact on the life of Peter French.

The boss of the Blitzen made a reputation for himself as a fence builder, as well as an irrigationist. Anyone who wanted to work at either fence building or ditch digging could find work at the P Ranch. The fences were often built between the rimrocks, a common geological feature of the country.

When "Old Man" (William) Barton decided to retire, French bought his place, which was just north of the Diamond Ranch and included Barton Lake, named for its owner. On this piece of land— atop a hill where it would be dry throughout the year—French built his famous round barn that still stands, a lasting tribute to his industry. The center post of the barn—a huge old juniper tree—

holds braces for the central roof, and a circle of posts supports the sloping dome of the roof. The outside wall holds up the ends of the long rafters.

A stone wall forms a central circular corral where horses could be roped, snubbed, saddled, and ridden—by buckaroos able to suppress their fear of riding wild horses inside. Here and on the track between the outer wall and the inner corral, horses were ridden till they seemed gentle.

French's theory was that, in this barn, colts could be broken in winter and be ready for riding when spring came, but his theory did not always work out. A horse could be ridden several days around the track inside the barn and seem gentle, yet might buck like a wild horse when mounted outside — a peculiarity of equine psychology that had to be learned from experience. However, the round barn made it possible for dozens of men to be occupied in the winters—and the job of breaking out a bunch of colts is better done when other work is not pressing. Cow horses rarely last long, and of the nearly three hundred head of horse and mule colts French raised each year, he kept about two-thirds on the ranch. The others were sold.

The late eighties were rather lean years for the cattle business in Southeast Oregon. The dry cycle that began in 1870 had continued. Though these dry years made the Blitzen Valley safer for livestock, they also made the adjacent ranges less productive of grass. This meant poorer beef and eventually fewer cattle. The cattle business had other problems. Railroads had been built to the Pacific Coast, and there was no longer demand for beef to feed railroad workers. On top of this, the Montana and Wyoming ranges had been stocked. Prices were down.

In a way, it was lucky for French that he sold heavily to help the Glenn estate in 1883-1886, even though this affected his income in later years. There was no letup in the demands of N. D. Rideout, who was valiantly trying to make the widespread business of the great promoter pay enough to satisfy the many insistent creditors, whose notes were drawing from ten to twelve per cent interest.

In 1889, French paid $7,755.40 for cattle and made sales of $82,202. In 1890, he bought $4,891.75 and sold $66,129.11; in 1891, he bought $8,675.50 and sold $51,145.54. By 1893, the figures were $9,940 and $79,826.51. There was not, however, much profit in this kind of market because of the huge expenses of ranch operations. Digging irrigation ditches, building fences, and making other improvements was a costly business.

Hundreds of men were on the French-Glenn payroll during peak seasons. Besides the crews working on developments, there was the crew of regular buckaroos who kept tab on the 45,000 head of cattle that had to be watched, branded, separated, and driven to market. The market was either at the old shipping point of Winnemucca, Nevada; or at Ontario, Oregon, after the railroad came to that town. Occasionally French had his cattle driven as far north as the Columbia River. His was a big outfit, and it stayed big even through the bad years because there was feed for the cattle and the debt was manageable. French himself made trips to San Francisco and back to Chicago with trainloads of cattle. Returning, he brought ever better bulls to constantly improve P Ranch cows.

So, during the lean years, the boss of the Blitzen managed to stay solvent—even prosper—while ranchers around him were going broke.

GLOOMY PREDICTIONS AT THE MARRIAGE OF PETER and Ella French came true just eight years later. On February 26, 1891, she sued for divorce, stating "the plaintiff alleges willful and constant desertion without cause on the part of the defendant." Peter French was alleged to have deserted her on January 1, 1889.

French—then in Chico, on business—received official notice on March 2. It would seem that the suit had been planned to coincide with one of his visits to California. In the complaint, Ella asked that her maiden name be restored but no note of that was made in the judge's decree.

Because, after her father's death, she chose to remain in Oakland with her widowed mother — rather than continue on to the P Ranch with Peter—the cattleman returned to Oregon alone—and that is the way he remained. Ella was born to the city; Peter to the country, and neither was ever willing to yield a way of life that had been happy and satisfying. Nor apparently was there ever any great love between them to resolve the differences.

That same year, 1883, that had witnessed her marriage to Peter and the death of her father, also saw the birth of her son, Harold Glenn French, on September 22, in Oakland. Harold was a blond boy with a touch of his mother's red coloring. Certainly he bore no resemblance to the black-haired, dark-eyed Peter French. In beautiful Spencerian handwriting, the divorce decree gave stipulations regarding the child: Ella was to have charge of him till he reached the age of twelve. After that, his time was to be divided equally between his mother and French, but neither was to remove

141

him from the state of California without the specific consent of the other. This, of course, prevented the boy from visiting his father except as Ella wished. The document expressed concern for the boy's health, which might have been poor, inasmuch as he had to have a regular physician. As for education, he was to be sent to a good college, one equal to the University of California. The arrangements were all very formal, very legal, very indicative of the trouble that comes from mismating, and—on French's part—from doing without a lawyer.

On April 9, 1891, shortly after she had obtained her divorce from French, Ellen married a bookkeeper by the name of Charles Lee Leonard. Two years later, the Glenns—or the creditors—decided to incorporate the French-Glenn outfit. Since French was the only one who knew anything about cows or how to manage a ranch, he was made president. By this time his one-third interest had dwindled considerably; he now held only one-fifth of the company stock. Papers of incorporation were filed with the Secretary of State of California on January 20, 1894. These papers constitute a rare document. No more thorough job of removing power and property from a man could have been accomplished without use of lethal weapons. Peter French was the man.

Signing the articles of incorporation were: Peter French with 20,000 shares worth $100,000; Ella and Frank and Charles Glenn, each with 23,058 shares, worth $115,290; Alice A. Young with 10,281 shares worth $54,105, and F. C. Lusk with 5 shares worth $25.

Lusk was secretary and the others, except Alice A. Young, a niece of the Glenns, were directors. The corporation lasted until November 30, 1910, when it forfeited its right to do business in California. Reasons for the formation of the French-Glenn Livestock Company are obscure. It did reduce the proportion French might have been entitled to under the original agreement with Dr. Glenn; the Glenn boys might have wanted to reduce the amount Ella would receive; or possibly the creditors and Lusk wanted closer control and assurance that the major income from the P and

Diamond Ranches would come to the Glenn estate. None could have been so foolish as to want control of the ranches taken from Peter French, long recognized as one of the most remarkable managers of a cow outfit in the entire West.

FRENCH-GLENN VS. ALVA SPRINGER

HAD THE DISPUTE BEEN SETTLED IN CONFORMITY with English common law, which gives the owner of a shore land the additional ownership of land to the middle, or center thread, of a stream or lake, then French-Glenn's claim would surely have been upheld. Or, if Peter French and the Glenns had known about riparian or shore rights earlier, there likely would never have been a court trial. But knowledge about riparian rights came late to both French and the Glenns. Settlers filtered into the area between French-Glenn land and Malheur Lake, with no opposition from the big company.

As long as the lake filled to the original meander line every year, there was no cause for controversy. Settlers would have found no land between French-Glenn and the lake water. But dry years, the breaching of the Sand Reef that permitted Malheur to drain into Harney, and French's own irrigation projects in the Blitzen Valley, all combined to lower the Malheur. This resulted in thousands of acres of exposed and unsurveyed land between the deeded property of French-Glenn and the official water line of the lake.

In the early eighties, French expressed no authority over lands beyond the meander line and it must be assumed that he felt kindly toward the men who were living there. Some of them even worked on his ranch when he needed help digging his irrigation ditches. French later testified that he expected to sell them water from his ditches along the Blitzen. Then these friendly relations between French and the settlers suddenly ceased.

One day in 1894, French returned from a meeting of the French-Glenn Livestock Company and immediately sat down at his desk to write letters to all the settlers beyond the meander line. There, in the lonely white house beneath the blowing poplars, he informed them that the land on which they lived belonged to the company.

The letter to settler Alva Springer—typical of them all—read:

P Ranch, Aug. 24, '94

Mr. Alva Springer

Narrows,

Dear Sir,

    As riparian owners, and under the rulings of the Land Department, the decision of the Supreme Court, we are the legal owners of the unsurveyed lands bordering on, and lying north of our lands in township 26 south, range 31 east, of which the unsurveyed lands occupied by you are a portion.

    We respectfully ask that you make some other arrangement as to the further occupancy of said lands, and for the use or removal of the crop of hay growing thereon.

Very Respectfully Yours

(Signed) Peter French

There were dozens of such letters sent out by French, as general manager of the French-Glenn Livestock Company, in compliance with the decision of the stockholders at their recent meeting. When the settlers paid no attention to them, French started suits in the Federal court in Portland. These suits were transferred to the circuit court at Burns. Testimony shows that French asked the settlers to choose one case which would decide the entire controversy and make it cheaper for them. Though they did not comply, the French-Glenn vs. Springer case became the test case.

For nearly three years—from the time the letters were sent till the opening of the trial, May 24, 1897 — relations between Peter French and the settlers steadily deteriorated until there was a bitter enmity between them, especially on the part of the settlers. They were in danger of losing their only bit of security, of being driven from their pitiful little homes. They held meetings, listened to impassioned speakers, hired lawyers, and joined in what was to them a Holy War to save their homes. They were united in a common hatred of Peter French.

French, no talker, spread no propaganda.

The transcript of evidence of the French-Glenn vs. Springer case shows M. D. Clifford as judge, Lionel R. Webster and John Cummins as attorneys for Springer, and Charles W. Parrish and Thornton Williams as attorneys for French-Glenn. It is a famous case in Oregon. The plaintiff's attorneys presented the documents showing ownership of the fractional lots lying immediately south of the meander line in Section 26 South, Range 31 East of the Willamette Meridian. They had been purchased from the state as swamp land by W. Allen and C. E. Preston in 1889 and 1890, and sold to Peter French in 1890 for $675. Proof of the location of the meander line was given. After opening statements, Peter French was put on the stand, and remained there the better part of three days.

French testified to the formation of the company, to his presidency of it, and to the fact that he was general manager of it. He showed familiarity with the country where he had lived for twenty-five years. He was certain there was more water in Malheur Lake before the Sand Reef was breached and also before he started his irrigation program, which took water from the Blitzen to irrigate the bottom land in that valley. All these physical facts seemed indisputable.

The defendant's attorneys based their case on testimony showing that there was no actual lake for a distance of several miles north of the meander land. If there were no lake, they argued, the owner of the abutting land could not claim ownership of the intervening lands. There was little testimony regarding riparian law, though the plaintiff's lawyers did state that it made no difference whether the lake had receded from natural causes or from some act of man.

French testified that Springer had built on a knoll, had cut hay, and had deprived him of use of the land which he considered to be worth fifty cents per acre to French-Glenn. He also testified that he had demanded possession of the land numerous times. Springer claimed that French had encouraged him to settle.

The case closed after seven days of heated and conflicting testimony. Such differing evidence is not strange in cases at law, and the function of juries is to sort out the true from the false by the attitude of the witnesses and their reputations for veracity. Judge Clifford did that which is common to judges: he presented statements from both sides as a charge to the jury. On his own, he summed up the evidence:

> "The principal question for you to decide, gentlemen of the jury, is a question of fact, and that fact is, whether or not these lands upon which the defendant has settled, and is settled at the present time, are lands included in the adjoining tract of land described by the plaintiff in this case, and to which the plaintiff claims title; and which they claim belong to this land by virtue of these extending lines, or accretions, as they call it, which extend into this lake which is called Malheur Lake."

In other words, did the receding waters of Malheur Lake, by riparian right, extend the boundaries of the plaintiff's lands—or open a new region for settlers? Common law would have brought in a verdict for French-Glenn. The jury in the circuit court at Burns decided in favor of the defendant, Alva Springer.

General sentiment was against the company. Business men wanted the settlers to stay, and the many poor men on homesteads or claims throughout Harney County's 10,132 square miles wanted the small men to win. Possibly the settlers won the case because there were more of them.

THE BATTLE CONTINUES

DESPITE THE VERDICT, THE LOT OF THE SETTLERS was far from a happy one. This was stock, not agricultural, country, which meant that settlers had to raise cattle or sheep or horses, and it is doubtful if cattlemen would have put up with sheep or sheepmen in Harney County any longer than they did in Crook or Grant counties, where there was wholesale slaughter of sheep by cattlemen.

To run cattle, settlers had to compete with the big stockmen—of whom French was but one—and these established, often ruthless, men did not relish competition. They had come to believe the grass was theirs by right of discovery. French did draw a more explosive type of settler at the mouth of the Blitzen than homesteaded on surveyed land in other parts of the county, and he was less violent than many other stockmen in protecting his grass. There are desert waterholes in Harney County where more men have been killed in stockmen's quarrels than in all the Blitzen Valley. Peter French went to law.

Though French permitted settlers to run their cattle on his land, he liked to have a man present when they took their cattle out. He did let them use his bulls, though the boss of the P Ranch was not so philosophical about that as Henry Miller, who bought extra bulls for the small farmers surrounding his ranches. However, Miller was a butcher, and it made no difference to him whose cow produced the meat he sold. French had good bulls, Shorthorns for years, but there is a record of his paying $1,100 to John Catlow for two Hereford bulls, which must have been a very high price at the end of the nineteenth century.

148

The fact is that French was the scapegoat of the settlers, an individual on whom they could blame their troubles, an excuse for their bad luck and worse judgment. His defeat in the French-Glenn vs. Springer case certainly elated most of them. Some even hoped to press on with further humiliation. That is the way people are: forgiving or vindictive. As for French himself, he had little to say; he was too busy to spend time on public relations. Peter French expressed himself in action. If he learned that a family was short of meat in the winter, he would send half a beef over to them— but more often the settler took care of that problem himself. French contributed to the schools and supported the school near the Sod House, for he was almost the only landowner in the area; but he no longer met with the settlers, nor did he attend their social functions, their dances, or their spelling bees. Settlers worked for him at haying and ditching and draining, but his work was seasonal and his contact with the men sporadic.

The French-Glenn Company made no movement to withdraw the suits against settlers, other than Springer; and when it was learned that that case would be appealed to a higher court, resentment against French became stronger, dividing settlers into several groups. They all hated French but proposed different methods of retaliation. Some moved away, some merely talked and blustered, some stole more grass and cattle; the dangerous ones plotted violence, unwilling to trust the law.

The group that met to plot the physical, rather than the legal, destruction of Peter French did not have the support of all the settlers, nor even a majority, but they spoke at every meeting and tried to inflame others. Gangs were organized to move at night, cutting French-Glenn fences, sometimes for miles, without leaving evidence that could lead to arrest. They mixed the cattle and caused such harassment that the big ranch expense account was raised beyond normal figures.

Ed Oliver lived just east of the Rock Ford on a homestead. His trouble with French was different; he had petitioned for a road and felt that it had been denied by the county court through action by French. He had married a Simmons girl and was father of a growing family. Oliver was a very small man, no larger than Peter French. Owner of but a few head of stock, he helped his mother-in-law look after her herd. Ed Oliver was certain that all his troubles stemmed from this big landowner for whom he had worked during haying for several summers.

It must be said that the mental condition of Peter French was not one to engender calm. The French-Glenn Livestock Company had taken financial control of the ranch away from him. This gave the Glenn heirs the right to countermand his orders. In addition to this, the price of cattle had dropped; the demands of the Glenns for money hampered his management; the settlers were a constant nuisance; his wife had left him and married another man; and the boy who bore his name—and had visited him that summer—was, at the age of fourteen, spoiled and self-centered. Worst of all, he was a reddish blond with no physical resemblance to French himself. Though French was a man to keep his troubles to himself, he was no less bitter.

The frustrations of the cattleman matched those of the settlers. They were bound to clash.

MURDER ON SAGEBRUSH FLAT

PETER FRENCH RETURNED FROM A BUSINESS TRIP to Chicago on Christmas Day of 1897. In Burns, he had Mart Brenton at the livery stable hook his team onto the buckboard, which was loaded with gifts he had bought for the children of his crew. He then drove directly to the Sod House Ranch. That night there was a Christmas party, with all the children happy over the holiday and the men and women in festive mood. Chino Berdugo, boss of the drive that was to start the next day, had fallen ill. French directed him to take the buckboard and team and go on to the P Ranch, where he could rest until he felt better.

On the morning of December 26, French took Chino's horse and assumed the role of boss of the crew. Finding the horse a little slow, he stopped and cut a rod of willow, with which to aid his spurs. Later he attached a string of buckskin to the willow, to make a whip for urging the cattle on. They moved slowly in the cold weather of the winter day.

As they approached the gate to the big sagebrush field, French rode around the cattle to open the gate. Throwing it back and remounting, he entered the field so that the cattle would follow. Suddenly he saw Ed Oliver ride out of a swale with his horse at a gallop. Oliver headed straight for French and charged full tilt. The horses clashed together so hard that French's mount went to its knees. French struck Oliver's horse over the head in an effort to fend Oliver off. According to Emanuel Clark—one of French's riders and the man nearest the scene—Oliver charged French again and French then struck him over the head and shoulders with his willow whip.

151

Oliver pulled his gun from his waistband and waved it. French rode a few yards away, then looked back. As he did so, Oliver fired, hitting the boss of the P Ranch in the right cheek. The bullet passed through French's head to emerge behind his left ear. He was killed instantly. Oliver rode past his body, which lay on the ground, and headed west at a fast clip. He likely feared vengeance from the French crew.

There was no danger. The men were shocked by the sudden death of their friend and leader, but they were unarmed. Some wept, and a few warned others not to touch the body till the coroner arrived. The body was merely covered with some remnants of saddle blankets until night, when Andrea Littrell, who lived at the Sod House, brought a tent to place over the body.

The murder occurred about two o'clock in the afternoon. The coroner, T. W. Stephens, came the next day to take charge of the body. After the coroner had made his observations, Mart Brenton took the remains to the upstairs living quarters of Leon Brown of Burns, a long-time friend of French. There, above the Brown store, Dr. W. L. Marsden conducted his examination, which resulted in his testimony to the jury.

Dr. Marsden—an old friend and admirer of French—removed the brain from the skull and weighed it. It came to sixty-four ounces, one of the largest brains ever put on scales. The bullet had entered the right side of the face, coursing through the brain in a slightly upward and backward direction.

On December 28, Mart Brenton and Burt French—the brother of the murdered man—started by team for Baker City, with the body in a zinc-lined box. There the body was embalmed and shipped by Wells Fargo Express to Red Bluff, California. The funeral was held on January 4, 1898, in Red Bluff, followed by interment in the Oak Hill Cemetery there, where French's father and mother were buried. The stone column that marks his grave bears only the name "Peter French," and the dates of his birth and death.

Dave Crow, a rider for the P Ranch, had witnessed the murder. Within minutes he started for Winnemucca to notify the world that probably its best-known cowman had been killed. He rode first to the P Ranch to change horses, then headed out over the trail south that led through Fields, at the lower end of the Steens. Crow changed horses nine times during the trip, commandeering a new mount when the one he was riding tired and a new one was available. He reached Winnemucca in forty-three hours without resting. Meanwhile a coroner's jury had convened at the Sod House Ranch and found that Peter French met death from gunshot wounds inflicted by Ed L. Oliver.

Newspapers gave generous space to the killing of this well-known man, but some of the stories were distorted because of scant information. The Burns paper, which had seldom spoken favorably of French, covered the murder in a few words on an inside page. This was a forerunner of the caution with which many Harney County residents still discuss the killing of Peter French. After nearly three-quarters of a century, it still remains a controversial subject, and information about it is colored by the individual prejudice of the teller. The Burns newspaper defended the county against a charge by the *Oregonian* that the $10,000 bail for Oliver had been set too low, adding that local sentiment seemed to favor the culprit. Indictment of Oliver was made on a charge filed by Burt French, and bail was furnished by Fred Lunaberg, Burns merchant; H. B. Simmons, Narrows farmer; N. J. Simmons, Narrows farmer; A. S. Ward, Smith farmer; H. M. Horton, Burns druggist; W. D. Huffman, Diamond farmer, and J. B. Craig, Riley farmer.

Oliver had a short police record, having been arrested once in Harney County, on October 29, 1894, when he was charged with assault with a dangerous weapon—a long-handled shovel—and with beating one Samuel Handley with said shovel, by striking him in and upon the body and limbs. The indictment was declared faulty and was dismissed, but another indictment followed. Then Oliver's attorney filed a demurrer and the case was dropped.

Ed Oliver's original indictment for the murder of Peter French was dropped the day before the trial, probably by some agreement between the attorneys. On May 18, Oliver was charged with manslaughter. Possibly the district attorney, Charles W. Parrish, felt more confident of winning the lighter charge. Oliver's trial began on May 19, 1898, at Burns. Money had been raised for his defense from among those who were glad that French was gone. The directing defense attorney was Lionel R. Webster, who had defended Alva Springer the year before. Webster had previously been a member of the firm of Carey, Idleman, Mays & Webster, of Portland, until that firm dissolved and Idleman and Webster became partners.

Emanuel Clark was the opening witness for the prosecution. He testified that Oliver's horse ran into French's and that French motioned with his whip as if directing Oliver to leave the property. He stated that French then rode westward, with Oliver following; that Oliver raised his right arm and lowered it, raised it again and fired.

Dave Crow testified that he saw the shooting, saw the men come together, and watched while French tried to drive Oliver away. He also stated that French turned west, with Oliver following. Prim Ortego, who had been with French since 1877, likewise witnessed the murder. He had been about two hundred yards away and described the scene much as did Crow and Clark.

French's younger brother Burt stated that he too saw Peter open the gate and ride away from it, saw Oliver gallop up to him and refuse to turn back when ordered to do so. He recalled that Peter said, "I will drive you off," and that Oliver reached for a pistol as his brother rode away.

According to Burt French, "Oliver snapped the pistol and my brother turned his head and Oliver fired again and my brother fell." He did not see his brother strike Oliver.

Sheriff John McKinnon testified that he had arrested Ed Oliver on December 27, at Mrs. Simmons' place, and that Oliver had the pistol at the house. "He had it in his waistband. I asked him for it and he gave it to me, saying it was the one he used."

Andrea Littrell saw the pockets of the dead man examined and reported there were no weapons. Dr. Walter L. Marsden testified about the wound and about the clothing worn by French, which included a heavy overcoat buttoned except for the top button, a broad belt buckled over the overcoat, gloves, overshoes, and a scarf about the neck. He also testified that there were no weapons on the body—except a small, unopened pocket knife.

Webster, for the defense, was a more experienced lawyer than Parrish, and surely more informed about the human race. Like Jackson Hatch, when he defended Huram Miller for the murder of Dr. Glenn, Webster built a case around fear of bodily injury as a reason for the murder. In neither trial was there any doubt of the murderer; both acts had been done in broad daylight and before witnesses. Webster prepared his case from the testimony of men who swore that French had abused Oliver with threats over a period of years. He clearly intimated that Oliver feared the big landowner—and Parrish failed to counter with the easily proved fact that Oliver's fears did not keep him from trespassing on French-Glenn property, nor from meeting with leaders among the settlers who wanted French destroyed.

There was no reference to the oft-repeated story that three or more men met and agreed that French must be killed, and drew straws to see who would do it, and that Oliver agreed to substitute for the man who drew the fatal straw, but lost his nerve.

During her testimony, Mrs. Ed Oliver said that the family had been up late Christmas night and had slept later than usual the next morning, breakfast having been eaten around ten o'clock. Her husband had left the house about one o'clock to tend the cattle, returning home around sundown. The sheriff had come the following day.

Just about one hour after Ed Oliver left his house, Peter French was dead. His partner, Hugh Glenn, had been struck down at the same hour, just fourteen years before.

The defense tried to prove that French carried a large stick with which he hit Oliver, but anyone reading the notes of the county clerk, taken at the trial, would not have been impressed with the quality of that evidence.

During his turn on the stand, Oliver said that he had lived at Rock Ford nine years and owned no land in dispute with the French-Glenn Livestock Company. He testified that he left home, on December 26, at about eleven o'clock, went to George Curtis's, and stayed there until after dinner, then started for Rock Ford and his place. He thus contradicted his wife's testimony. He also denied having knowledge of French's return from Chicago.

According to Oliver, French carried a stick, which he feared was a whipstock, and began beating him with it. He declared that French said "I'll kill you!" and reached for a gun. At that moment, Oliver said he jerked his own pistol and fired as quickly as possible—afraid that French would kill him.

By the end of the trial, Attorney Webster had called on all his abilities—which in his case were considerable. During his plea to the jury, he had Mrs. Oliver, with her youngest child in her arms, sit before the jurymen while he tearfully described what a fine husband and father Oliver was, and what a crime it would be to divide this happy household, which the "brave defendant" had risked his life to preserve. The jury was out only three hours. At seven o'clock, in the dusk of a late May evening, the foreman announced a verdict of "Not Guilty."

In death as in life, Peter French lost to the settlers in a court of law.

F. C. LUSK, SECRETARY OF THE FRENCH-GLENN
Livestock Company, was named executor of Peter French's will,
which was admitted to probate, January 21, 1898, in San Francisco.
The will stated that the deceased left no widow and the only heir
was Harold G. French of Jacinto. The boy was then fourteen.

French's personal estate consisted of $20,000 in San Francisco
banks, capital stock in the French-Glenn Livestock Company worth
around $20,000, and real estate in San Jose, valued at about $2,500.
The will charged the executor to pay all just and honest debts; to
give his three aunts, on his mother's side, the house and lot he had
bought for them; and to convert the rest of the estate into cash,
one quarter of which was to go to the aunts, the rest to be held in
trust for Harold.

As for the real property, there were 3,265.14 acres in the name
of Peter French, some clear and some mortgaged to E. C. Singletary and the German Loan and Savings Society, money lenders
with whom French and Glenn as well as the French-Glenn Livestock Company had done much business. Acting in his capacity as
attorney for French-Glenn, the many-sided Lusk came into court
and claimed title to all this land for the company, starting suit to
prove it. No one opposed him, and, on March 28, 1900, he won
the case by default; at that time, French-Glenn (now, all Glenn)
took possession of the land.

Lusk thus became ranch manager, in addition to being executor
of both the Peter French and the Hugh Glenn estates, N. D. Rideout
having died. How he handled these properties cannot be explained

from existing books, but he did eventually pay off all the debts of the estates and he did keep the Glenn family living in the lavish style to which they were accustomed. It was during his administration that the famous P brand gave way to the FG brand.

In 1906, Lusk sold the P and Diamond ranches to Henry L. Corbett, who was later to become a Senator of Oregon—prominent in both the politics and business of the state. Purchase price of the big ranch was estimated at $300,000. At this time it was no longer a going concern; all the cattle had been sold previously.

After the sale, Lusk turned the administration of the estate over to Charles N. Glenn, the doctor's oldest living son. In 1908—a little more than twenty-five years after the doctor had been killed— Charles divided the estate among the three remaining Glenns: Ella, 46; Frank, 44; and himself, 49. His final account showed $38,072.06.

Ella and her husband, Charles Leonard, continued to live on the Jacinto Ranch, until his death in the late 1920's, whereupon she moved into the Barton Hotel in Willows. By now most of her money was gone and her expensive habits necessarily curtailed. In Willows, she lived a quiet life, spending a part of nearly every day in the local library. She never talked about her personal affairs.

"She was," say those who knew her during these lean years, "not a woman you could ask questions of."

Newspapers noted that now and then Harold visited his mother for a day or two at a time. He was living in San Francisco, on the income from the estate of Peter French, which was held in a trust fund for him. Then, suddenly, he died with no warning—other than a history of never having been strong physically. He was found dead in his room, Thursday morning, February 26, 1936, aged 53. There was a private funeral and the body was sent to Oakland for cremation.

Inheriting the trust fund from her son, Ella moved to San Francisco. There, on November 21, 1938—less than three years after the death of Harold—she herself died, while a resident of the Western Woman's Club on Sutter Street. She also was cremated in the city of Oakland, to which her life had been linked in so many ways. That California community had witnessed her years of splendor, her ill-starred marriage to the Oregon cowman, and the birth of her only child.

Up in Oregon, things were not going so well for the settlers at Malheur Lake. They found that the death of Peter French did not solve their problems; they had merely killed their scapegoat and now had to assume responsibility for their own ills. There was still the same limitation on the variety of crops possible; the railroad was just as far away, and transportation just as slow. Competition with the large stockmen had not abated, nor competition with one another. But they held onto their land, living on it when the water was not too high, until they finally acquired a sort of title by adverse possession—a title similar to that obtained by squatters in earlier days; in fact, similar to the right of the old-time stockmen.

More and more, the settlers fell to quarreling among themselves. Some who held land abutting the meander line tried to invoke the law of riparian rights and exclude others who had settled beyond it. There was an active association of riparian owners of Malheur Lake, whose existence can be considered a vindication of the attitude of French-Glenn, inasmuch as the very group that killed French followed the same course he had been killed for inaugurating.

The decision of the jury in the French-Glenn vs. Springer case was made when water was lapping the foundations of settlers' houses, and—ironically enough—was to the effect that there was no lake; therefore there were no accretions under riparian law. Legally, an accretion is the acquisition of land through the gradual action of natural forces. This can include the recession of water from a given watermark. In *accretion,* the added or acceded land belongs to the owner of the adjacent land, thereby extending his boundaries.

Nevertheless, after many years, the supreme court of Oregon and the supreme court of the United States affirmed the original judgment in the French-Glenn vs. Springer case. When the decision was finally handed down, Peter French was long dead from an act of violence whose flame was fanned during the original trial of this case. In fact, from the date of the trial, events moved inevitably, and with a kind of destined order, to the final crime of Ed Oliver. As for the settlers themselves, by the time the supreme courts finally decided in favor of Springer, they had little interest in the case. The rosy glow of anticipation that shone when they raised money to help Alva Springer keep his land and Ed Oliver escape punishment had proved a false dawn.

Though Peter French appealed to the courts, rather than resort to the violent methods used by many big stockmen, he lost his cases in both life and death. He lost twice to Springer, when common law was in his favor; and his murderer was judged "Not Guilty."

Oliver himself grew increasingly arrogant, attempting to bask in the role of public benefactor; but the reaction of the more thoughtful and more moral element of the community prevailed, and he became unpopular. Eventually French-Glenn purchased his land. On October 11, 1898, his wife filed for, and received, a divorce. A year later she remarried, and with her new husband, lived a long and respected life in Eastern Oregon. Oliver finally left the country.

The passing years have proved that it took a man with the steel and stamina of the irreplaceable Peter French to run that cattle empire. Henry Corbett sold out to Swift & Company, and they in turn, finding the land unprofitable, in 1935, sold 64,717 acres to the Federal government for an addition to the Malheur National Wildlife Refuge. The purchase price was $675,000. The land the government obtained was almost identical with that owned by Peter French and Dr. Glenn. In 1908, President Theodore Roosevelt had set aside Malheur and Harney lakes as a refuge for the native wildfowl; that had been the beginning of the project.

The creation of the refuge did not greatly disturb the determined settlers along the Malheur. They could still lease grazing areas under the regulations imposed by the Department of the Interior. The chief restriction is that hay cannot be cut until the nesting season is over. Some say this gives the big, tough grass a chance to increase, to the detriment of the smaller and more nutritious grass the cattle will eat. After the establishment of the refuge, settlers asked the county to assess the land they occupied in order to show possession and pay taxes. Since then, a number of them have acquired sufficient title to hold legal possession of the land on which they live.

Today thousands of bird lovers—and hunters in season—visit the site of the old P Ranch, to observe, to study, and take pictures. Countless others are drawn to the Blitzen Valley by the romance of the early days when one man, through ambition and ability, carved a cattle kingdom, and was viciously murdered while still expanding that kingdom. Now, a small store and hotel called Frenchglen help to keep alive the memory of Peter French and his financial backer, Dr. Hugh James Glenn of California.

Here, in the valley of the Donner und Blitzen, almost a century ago, French set a pattern for modern cow ranches, with emphasis on improving the land and the cattle by the best scientific methods available. There are other valleys in Eastern Oregon, green with native grass, beautiful to the cowman and to cows, fertile, and well watered; yet none has the glamor French gave to the Blitzen by the intensity and single-mindedness of his efforts—the price he paid for his own ambition and his loyalty to Dr. Glenn.

Records:

Transcript: French-Glenn vs. Springer, Oregon Supreme Court Library; Transcript: State of Oregon vs. Oliver, Oregon Supreme Court Library; Testimony: United States vs. Oregon, U. S. Department of Interior; *Great Register*, Colusa County, California, 1872; Peter French's *Journal*, 1872-78; *Laws of California*, 1872; *Memoirs* of Maurice Fitzgerald; Clerk's Records in Harney County Courthouse, Burns, Oregon; Archives of State of Oregon, Salem, Oregon; California Prison Records, 1883; California Corporation Records, 1892; Records of Glenn Family in Bancroft Library, Berkeley, California; Probate of Hugh James Glenn Estate in Glenn County Courthouse, 1883 *et seq.*; *Yearbook of U. S. Department of Agriculture*, 1938; *Disposition of the Public Domain in Oregon*, U. S. Department of Interior; Records of Oregon State Land Board, Salem, Oregon; Assessor's Records, Harney County, Burns, Oregon.

Books:

George F. Brimlow, *Harney County, Oregon and Its Range Land*, Portland; Bernard DeVoto, *Across the Wide Missouri*, Boston, 1947; W. S. Green, *History of Colusa County, California*, 1950; Will James, *All in a Day's Riding*, New York, 1933; Burl Ives, *Burl Ives Song Book*, New York, 1953; Lewis A. McArthur, *Oregon Geographic Names*, Portland, 1944; McComish, *History of Colusa and Glenn Counties*, San Francisco, 1918; Anne Shannon Monroe, *Feelin' Fine*, 1930; Joseph C. Nimmo, *History of United States Cattle*, 1885; Herman Oliver, *Gold and Cattle Country*, Portland, 1961; Martin Schmitt, ed., *Autobiography of General George Crook*,

1960; Martin Schmitt, ed., *The Cattle Drives of David Shirk,* 1956; Edward Treadwell, *The Cattle King,* New York, 1931; Elizabeth Lambert Wood, *Pete French, Cattle King,* Portland, 1951; Jesse Walton Woolridge, *History of the Sacramento Valley,* 1931; Western Historical Publishing Company, *History of Central Oregon,* 1903; Western Historical Publishing Company, *Illustrated History of Baker, Grant, Malheur and Harney Counties,* 1904.

Newspaper Files:

Burns *Times-Herald;* Colusa *Sun;* Georgetown *Gazette;* Oakland *Tribune;* Placer County *Argus;* Portland *Oregon Journal;* Portland *Oregonian;* Red Bluff *Sentinel;* Sacramento *Daily Record;* San Francisco *Alta Californian;* San Francisco *Call;* San Francisco *Examiner;* Willows *Transcript.*

Magazine Files:

Fortnight, Magazine of the Pacific Coast; Oregon Cattleman; Oregon Historical Quarterly; Pacific Coast Review.

Interviews:

Mrs. Addah Bedford, Willows, California; William Bradeen, Burns, Oregon; Al Brown, Burns, Oregon; Man Bundy, Ontario, Oregon; Pat Cecil, Burns, Oregon; Elliott R. Corbett, Portland, Oregon; Chester Craddock, Harney County Judge; Silva Durkheimer, Portland, Oregon; Elizabeth Ewing, Willows, California; Mrs. Ernest French, Pendleton, Oregon; Nelson Higgs, Harney County Judge; Bertha Hossman, Burns, Oregon; W. H. Hutchinson, Chico, California; E. R. Jackman, Corvallis, Oregon; Grover Jameson, Burns, Oregon; R. E. Kriesien, Portland, Oregon; Rebecca Lambert, Willows, California; Hall S. Lusk, Salem, Oregon; L. A. McArthur, Willows, California; Leo A. McCoy, Red Bluff, California; Archie McGowan, Burns, Oregon; Herman Oliver, John Day, Oregon; W. B. Sale, Willows, California; John Scharff, Burns, Oregon; Berkeley Snow, Arch Cape, Oregon; Harold Warner, Salem, Oregon.

*This book was first printed in June 1964 by the
Metropolitan Printing Company of Portland, Oregon . . . Text com-
posed in linotype by Richard Gillson, using Caledonia, one of the
newer typefaces based on Scotch Modern, and created by
W. A. Dwiggins, eminent American graphic artist . . . Camera
production by Joseph W. Trager . . . Jacket art and endmap
by Harold Cramer Smith .*